THE SCHOOLS HISTORY PROJECT

S·H·P

OFFICIAL TEXT

# SOUTH AFRICA SINCE 1948

## a study in depth

**CORE TEXTS FOR GCSE**

**Christopher Culpin**

**Series Editors:
Christopher Culpin
Ian Dawson**

D1439674

**HODDER**
EDUCATION
AN HACHETTE UK COMPANY

# Acknowledgements

The Publishers would like to thank the following for permission to use copyright material:

**Photographs:**
**Cover** Gerald Hoberman © 1996; **p.2** *tl* Angela Hampton, *tr* Richard Greenhill/Sally & Richard Greenhill Photo Library, *bl* Sally Greenhill/Sally & Richard Greenhill Photo Library, *br* Sally & Richard Greenhill Photo Library; **p.3** *clockwise from tl* Richard Greenhill/Sally & Richard Greenhill Photo Library, Sally Greenhill/Sally & Richard Greenhill Photo Library, Angela Hampton, Sally & Richard Greenhill Photo Library, Richard Greenhill/Sally & Richard Greenhill Photo Library, Sally & Richard Greenhill Photo Library, © Syda Productions - Fotolia; **p.6** *tl* © Friedrich von Hörsten/Images of Africa Photobank, *tr & br* © David Keith Jones/Images of Africa Photobank, *c & bl* © Johann van Tonder/Images of Africa Photobank; **p.7** *all* David Keith Jones/Images of Africa Photobank; **p.10** Courtesy Library of Parliament, Cape Town; **p.12** Courtesy MuseuMAfricA, Johannesburg; **p.13** Courtesy MuseuMAfricA, Johannesburg; **p.16** *t* Courtesy MuseuMAfricA, Johannesburg, *c* Courtesy The William Fehr Collection, Cape Town, *b* Hulton Getty; **p.18** *t* Courtesy MuseuMAfricA, Johannesburg, *b* © Friedrich von Hörsten/Images of Africa Photobank; **p.20** Courtesy MuseuMAfricA, Johannesburg; **p.21** War Museum of the Boer Republics, Bloemfontein; **p.22** Topham Picturepoint; **p.24** *tl & tr* Hulton Getty, *b* Topham Picturepoint; **p.25** Popperfoto; **p.26** Topham Picturepoint; **p.27** Popperfoto; **p.28** Topham Picturepoint; **p.29** Topham Picturepoint; **p.30** *l* Courtesy MuseuMAfricA, Johannesburg, *r* Courtesy Neave Africana Collection/MuseuMAfricA, Johannesburg; **p.31** Courtesy MuseuMAfricA, Johannesburg; **p.33** Courtesy MuseuMAfricA, Johannesburg; **p.34** Courtesy Mayibuye Centre Photo Library, University of the Western Cape; **p.35** *l* Mary Evans Picture Library; **p.36** Courtesy MuseuMAfricA, Johannesburg; **p.37** Courtesy MuseuMAfricA, Johannesburg; **p.38** Courtesy Times Media Collection, MuseuMAfricA, Johannesburg; **p.39** Courtesy Times Media Collection/MuseuMAfricA, Johannesburg; **p.40** Courtesy MuseuMAfricA, Johannesburg; **p.42** *l* Associated Press, *r* Camera Press; **p.43** United Party, *Election News* (1948 pamphlet); **p.45** *tl* Associated Press, *tr* Terence Spencer/Camera Press, *bl* Popperfoto, *br* Courtesy Mayibuye Centre Photo Library, University of the Western Cape; **p.46** John Reader/Camera Press; **p.48** *t* Topham Picturepoint, *b* Orde Eliason/Link ©; **p.49** Rogan Coles/Link ©; **p.50** Oliphant ©1962 Pat Oliphant. Reprinted by permission of Universal Press Syndicate. All rights reserved.; **p.54** Popperfoto; **p.56** Times/Stephen Markeson/Camera Press; **p.57** *t* Orde Eliason/Link ©, *c* Courtesy Mayibuye Centre Photo Library, University of the Western Cape, *b* Greg English/Link ©; **p.64** *r* Rand Daily Mail/Times Media Limited; **p.67** Courtesy Mayibuye Centre Photo Library, University of the Western Cape; **p.68** Popperfoto; **p.69** Courtesy Mayibuye Centre Photo Library, University of the Western Cape; **p.71** Terence Spencer/Camera Press; **p.72** *l* © Wilf Schindler/Pixfeatures, *r* Courtesy Mayibuye Centre Photo Library, University of the Western Cape; **p.73** Eli Weinberg/Courtesy Mayibuye Centre Photo Library, University of the Western Cape; **p.75** Courtesy Mayibuye Centre Photo Library, University of the Western Cape; **p.76** Bailey's African History Archives/Link ©; **p.77** *l* I. Berry/Camera Press, *r* Courtesy Mayibuye Centre Photo Library, University of the Western Cape; **p.78** © Jürgen Schadeberg/South Photographs; **p.80** Courtesy Mayibuye Centre Photo Library, University of the Western Cape; **p.82** Courtesy Mayibuye Centre Photo Library, University of the Western Cape; **p.85** © Bailey's African History Archives/Link; **p.86** Michael Robbins/Courtesy Mayibuye Centre Photo Library, University of the Western Cape; **p.87** *t* Courtesy Mayibuye Centre Photo Library, University of the Western Cape, *b* Courtesy Mayibuye Centre Photo Library, University of the Western Cape; **p.88** Courtesy Mayibuye Centre Photo Library, University of the Western Cape; **p.89** Popperfoto; **p.91** © Sam Knox/Camera Press; **p.92** Courtesy Mayibuye Centre Photo Library, University of the Western Cape; **p.93** Courtesy Mayibuye Centre Photo Library, University of the Western Cape; **p.94** Topham Picturepoint; **p.98** David Goldblatt/South Photographs; **p.100** PA News Photo Library; **p.101** *t* PA News Photo Library, *b* Bodleian Library, Oxford (Rhodes House Library, the Anti-Apartheid Movement papers); **p.103** Greg English/Link ©; **p.105** *t* Courtesy Mayibuye Centre Photo Library, University of the Western Cape, *b* Anders Nilsson/AIM/Popperfoto; **p.106** Topham Picturepoint; **p.109** *t* Tom Blau/Camera Press, *bl* Greg English/Link ©, *br* Juhan Kuus/SIPA Press/Rex Features; **p.110–111** *t* Paul Weinberg/South Photographs, *b* Martine Velon/Camera Press; **p.112** *t* Orde Eliason/Link ©, *b* Greg English/Link ©; **p.114–115** Paul Weinberg/South Photographs/Link ©; **p.115** *r* Paul Weinberg/South Photographs/Link ©; **p.116** Martine Velon/Camera Press; **p.117** © Louise Gubb/JB Pictures/Network; **p.118** *t* Courtesy Mail & Guardian Publications; **p.119** Paul Weinberg/South Photographs/Link ©; **p.120** *l* Greg English/Link ©; **p.120-121** Popperfoto; **p.122** *t* Mykel Nicolaou/Link ©, *b* Popperfoto/Reuters; **p.124** Popperfoto/Reuters; **p.125** Anders Holmstrom/Courtesy Mayibuye Centre Photo Library, University of the Western Cape; **p.126** Associated Press/Topham; **p.128** John Parkin/Associated Press/Topham; **p.129** John Parkin/Associated Press/Topham; **p.130** *t* Photo Group/Link ©, *b* © Louise Gubb/Network **p.132** Popperfoto/Reuters; **p.134** *l* Popperfoto/Reuters; **p.134-5** Philip Schedler/Link ©; **p.135** *r* Popperfoto/Reuters; **p.136** Adil Bradlow/Associated Press.

**Written sources:**
**p.17** Nelson Mandela, *No Easy Walk to Freedom*, reprinted by permission of Heinemann Educational Publishers, a division of Reed Educational and Professional Publishing Ltd., 1965; **p.29 & p.31** Naboth Mokgatle, *Autobiography of an Unknown African*, C. Hurst & Co., 1971; **p.46** Extract from *Cape Times*, 13 December 1960; **p.47** Trevor Huddleston, *Naught for Your Comfort*, Collins, 1956; **p.58** Beverley Naidoo, *Journey to Jo'burg*, Collins, 1956; **p.64** (see p.17); **p.68** J. Pampallis, *Foundations of the New South Africa*, Maskew Millar Longman, 1991; **p.71** Albert Lutuli, *Let My People Go*, Collins, 1962; **p.72** H. Joseph, *Side by Side*, Zed Books; **p.73** Albert Lutuli, *Let My People Go*, Collins, 1962; **p.74** (see p.17); **p.75** Albert Lutuli, *Let My People Go*, Collins, 1962; **p.78** Albert Lutuli, *Let My People Go*, Collins, 1962; **p.81** Mary Benson, *Nelson Mandela*, Penguin, 1989; **p.86** Extract from *Cape Times*, 14 September 1977; **p.86** Lindy Wilson, *Bounds of Possibility*, Zed Books, 1991; **p.89** Lindy Wilson, *Bounds of Possibility*, Zed Books, 1991; **p.90** Julie Frederickse, *A Different Kind of War*, Ravan Press, 1986; **p.93** (see p.17); **p.105** Julie Frederickse, *A Different Kind of War*, Ravan Press, 1986; **p.106, p.113 & p.119** © Desmond Tutu, *The Rainbow People of God*, Transworld Publishers, 1994; **p.121** Extract from *Johannesburg Weekly Mail*, 1989; **p.133** Gerhard Marc and Georgina Hamilton, *An appetite for power: Buthelezi's Inkatha and the politics of loyal resistance*, Ravan Press; R Mkhondo, *Reporting South Africa*, Heinemann, 1993.

Every effort has been made to trace all copyright holders, but if any have been inadvertently overlooked the publishers will be pleased to make the necessary arrangements at the first opportunity.

Words printed in SMALL CAPITALS are defined in the Glossary on page 139.

© Christopher Culpin 2000

First published in 2000 by
Hodder Education, an Hachette Company
Carmelite House, 50 Victoria Embankment
London EC4Y 0DZ

Reprinted 2004, 2005, 2006, 2007, 2008, 2009, 2010, 2011, 2012 (twice), 2014, 2015, 2016, 2017

Layouts by Amanda Easter
Artwork by Art Construction, Linden Artists, Tony Randell
Typeset in 10.5/12pt Walbaum Book by Wearset, Boldon, Tyne and Wear
Colour separations by Colourscript, Mildenhall, Suffolk

Printed and bound in Dubai

A catalogue entry for this title is available from the British Library.

**ISBN-978 0 7195 7476 4**
Teachers' Resource Book ISBN 978 0 7195 74 77 1

# Contents

# INTRODUCTION

## **S**imilar or different?

Human beings are all more or less the same.

There are some obvious differences, such as gender

. . . and age

. . . and size

... and colour or race

or what language you speak ...

... and personality.

or how well off you are.

Some differences arise because of where you live ...

ALTHOUGH WE MAY look different, speak differently, and have different interests, scientists say that the similarities between us are far greater than the differences.

Nearly all our DNA, the biological 'building blocks' that make us who we are, is the same in all human beings (99.9999 per cent is the same; only 0.0001 per cent is different).

This book is about a place and a time when a government thought that differences in colour and race were very important, so important that they treated people differently for that reason alone. They built up a whole system, called APARTHEID, which separated people at work, at school and where they lived. Not only were people separated according to their race, but they were given different rights and treated unequally too.

THE PLACE WAS SOUTH AFRICA. THE TIME IS QUITE RECENT: THE YEARS SINCE 1948.

# The Universal Declaration of Human Rights

ON 10 DECEMBER 1948, the year apartheid began in South Africa, the UNITED NATIONS (UN) adopted the **Universal Declaration of Human Rights**. This was intended to be a measure by which people could judge whether a government treated its people properly. This summary of the 30 human rights in the Declaration is given here to help you judge what went on in South Africa in the years covered by this book. I hope it will help you judge other human rights situations too.

## ■ TASK

In some countries of the world, children as young as five years old are made to work. Either their parents are so poor that they need the money their children can earn, or they have sold their children to an employer to get money. These children work long hours, often in unsafe conditions, for low wages and have very little time off. Which of the human rights in the Declaration opposite are such children being deprived of?

**1 ALL HUMAN BEINGS ARE BORN FREE AND EQUAL IN DIGNITY AND RIGHTS.** They are endowed with reason and conscience and should act towards one another in a spirit of brotherhood.

**2** Everyone is entitled to all the rights and freedoms in this declaration without distinction of any kind, such as race, colour, sex, language, political or other opinion, national or social origin, property, birth or other status.

**3** Everyone has the right to life, liberty and security of person.

**4** No one shall be held in slavery.

**5** No one shall be subjected to torture or to cruel, inhuman or degrading treatment or punishment.

**6** Everyone has the right to be recognised as a person before the law.

**7** All are equal before the law and are entitled to equal protection before the law, without any discrimination.

**8** Everyone has the right to go to law to protect their rights.

**9** No one shall be subjected to arbitrary [unreasonable] arrest, detention or EXILE.

**10** Everyone is entitled to a fair trial, in public.

**11** Everyone accused of a crime in a court of law is presumed innocent until proved guilty in a public trial in which they have a right to defend themselves.

**12** No one shall be subjected to arbitrary interference with their privacy, family, home or correspondence, nor to attacks upon their honour and reputation.

**13** Everyone has the right of freedom of movement and residence within the borders of each state, and the right to leave and return freely to their country.

**14** Everyone has the right to seek ASYLUM from prosecution in other countries.

**15** Everyone has the right to a nationality.

**16** Men and women of full age have the right to marry and found a family without limitation due to race, nationality or religion.

17 Everyone has the right to own property.

18 Everyone has the right to freedom of thought, conscience and religion.

19 Everyone has the right to freedom of opinion and expression; this includes the right to receive and spread information and ideas in any media.

20 Everyone has the right to meet freely in peaceful organisations.

21 Everyone has the right to take part in the government of their country, either directly or through chosen representatives; everyone has the right of equal access to public services; the will of the people shall be the basis of government, expressed through regular elections, which shall be by universal and equal SUFFRAGE, held by secret vote.

22 Everyone has the right to the economic, social and cultural rights necessary for their dignity and free development of their personalities.

23 Everyone has the right to work, to free choice of employment, to just and favourable conditions of work; everyone has the right to equal pay for equal work; everyone has the right to fair pay, ensuring for themselves and their family a dignified existence.

24 Everyone has the right to rest and leisure, including reasonable hours and holidays with pay.

25 Everyone has the right to a standard of living adequate for the health and well-being of themselves and their family, including food, clothing, housing and medical care, and the right to security in the event of unemployment. Mothers and children are entitled to special care.

26 Everyone has the right to an education. Education shall be free and compulsory; access to higher education shall be on the basis of merit; education shall be directed towards the full development of the human personality, the strengthening of respect for human rights and freedoms. It shall promote understanding, tolerance and friendship among nations, racial or religious groups and shall further the activities of the UN for the maintenance of peace. Parents have the right to choose their child's education.

27 Everyone has the right to take part in the cultural life of the community, to enjoy the arts and share in the benefits of scientific advancement.

28 Everyone is entitled to a social and international order in which these rights can be realised.

29 Everyone has duties to the community; everyone is subject to the limitations of the law in order to respect the rights of others and meet the need for morality, public order and welfare.

30 Nothing in this declaration allows any state, group or person to destroy any of the rights or freedoms in it.

## ■ ACTIVITY

When you have read through the Declaration of Human Rights and understood it, keep a class 'Human Rights Diary': collect news items about events and situations in which people have been deprived of their human rights.

1. Keep a record of which rights people are being deprived of, where and when.
2. Which rights are people deprived of most often?
3. How do we find out about human rights abuses?
4. Which people or groups monitor the situation and report abuses to the world?

# South Africa: places and events

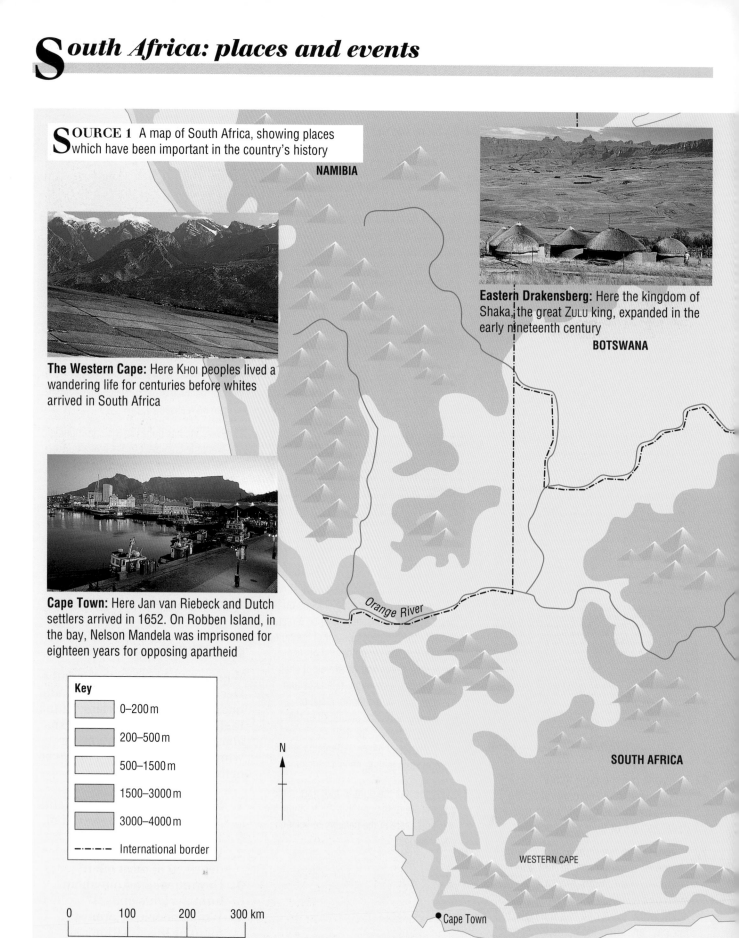

NAMIBIA

**Eastern Drakensberg:** Here the kingdom of Shaka, the great ZULU king, expanded in the early nineteenth century

BOTSWANA

**The Western Cape:** Here KHOI peoples lived a wandering life for centuries before whites arrived in South Africa

**Cape Town:** Here Jan van Riebeck and Dutch settlers arrived in 1652. On Robben Island, in the bay, Nelson Mandela was imprisoned for eighteen years for opposing apartheid

Orange River

SOUTH AFRICA

WESTERN CAPE

Cape Town

**Key**

| | |
|---|---|
| | 0–200 m |
| | 200–500 m |
| | 500–1500 m |
| | 1500–3000 m |
| | 3000–4000 m |
| –·–·–·– | International border |

N

0   100   200   300 km

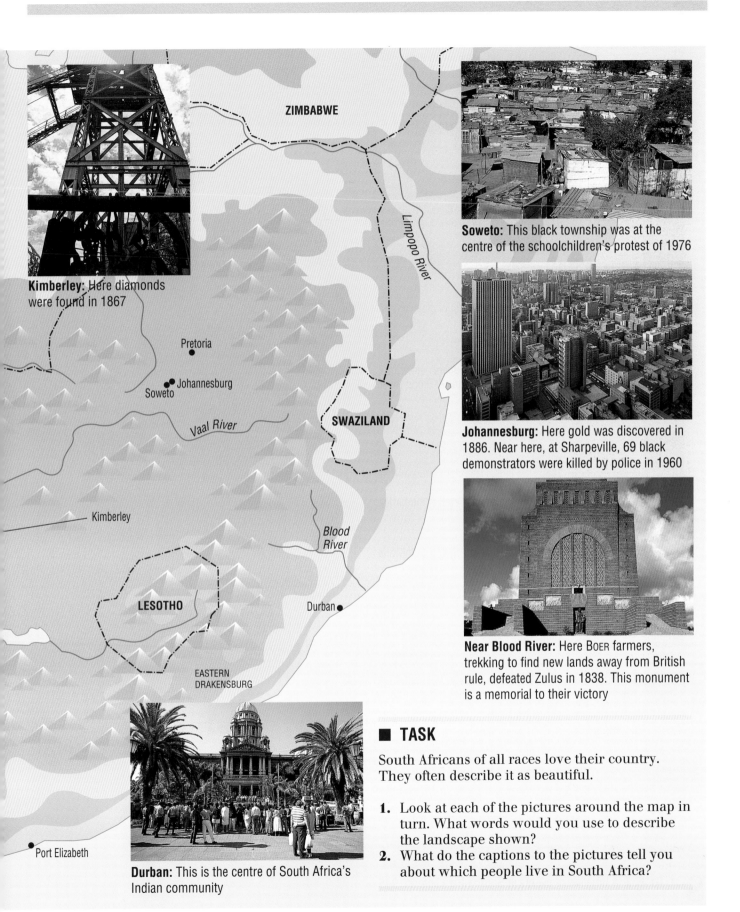

**Kimberley:** Here diamonds were found in 1867

**Soweto:** This black township was at the centre of the schoolchildren's protest of 1976

**Johannesburg:** Here gold was discovered in 1886. Near here, at Sharpeville, 69 black demonstrators were killed by police in 1960

**Near Blood River:** Here BOER farmers, trekking to find new lands away from British rule, defeated Zulus in 1838. This monument is a memorial to their victory

**Durban:** This is the centre of South Africa's Indian community

ZIMBABWE

Limpopo River

Pretoria

Johannesburg
Soweto

Vaal River

SWAZILAND

Kimberley

Blood River

LESOTHO

Durban

EASTERN DRAKENSURG

Port Elizabeth

### ■ TASK

South Africans of all races love their country. They often describe it as beautiful.

1. Look at each of the pictures around the map in turn. What words would you use to describe the landscape shown?
2. What do the captions to the pictures tell you about which people live in South Africa?

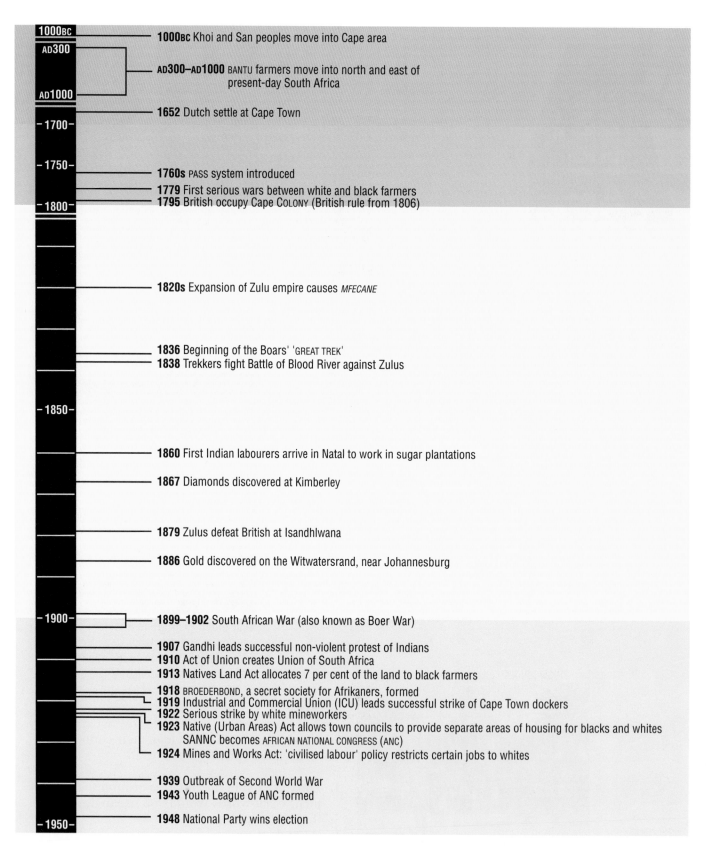

**1000BC** — **1000BC** Khoi and San peoples move into Cape area

**AD300** — **AD300–AD1000** BANTU farmers move into north and east of present-day South Africa

**AD1000**

— **1652** Dutch settle at Cape Town

−1700−

−1750− — **1760s** PASS system introduced

— **1779** First serious wars between white and black farmers

−1800− — **1795** British occupy Cape COLONY (British rule from 1806)

— **1820s** Expansion of Zulu empire causes *MFECANE*

— **1836** Beginning of the Boars' 'GREAT TREK'

— **1838** Trekkers fight Battle of Blood River against Zulus

−1850−

— **1860** First Indian labourers arrive in Natal to work in sugar plantations

— **1867** Diamonds discovered at Kimberley

— **1879** Zulus defeat British at Isandhlwana

— **1886** Gold discovered on the Witwatersrand, near Johannesburg

−1900− — **1899–1902** South African War (also known as Boer War)

— **1907** Gandhi leads successful non-violent protest of Indians

— **1910** Act of Union creates Union of South Africa

— **1913** Natives Land Act allocates 7 per cent of the land to black farmers

— **1918** BROEDERBOND, a secret society for Afrikaners, formed

— **1919** Industrial and Commercial Union (ICU) leads successful strike of Cape Town dockers

**1922** Serious strike by white mineworkers

**1923** Native (Urban Areas) Act allows town councils to provide separate areas of housing for blacks and whites
SANNC becomes AFRICAN NATIONAL CONGRESS (ANC)

— **1924** Mines and Works Act: 'civilised labour' policy restricts certain jobs to whites

— **1939** Outbreak of Second World War

— **1943** Youth League of ANC formed

−1950− — **1948** National Party wins election

**S**OURCE 2  A timeline of events in South Africa before 1948

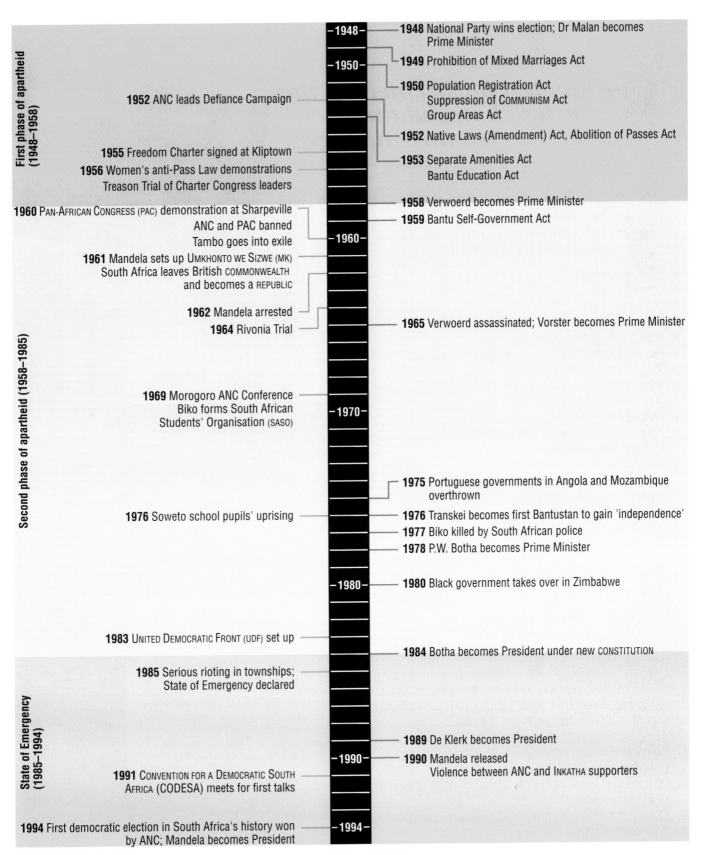

**First phase of apartheid (1948–1958)**

**1952** ANC leads Defiance Campaign

**1955** Freedom Charter signed at Kliptown
**1956** Women's anti-Pass Law demonstrations
Treason Trial of Charter Congress leaders

**1960** PAN-AFRICAN CONGRESS (PAC) demonstration at Sharpeville
ANC and PAC banned
Tambo goes into exile
**1961** Mandela sets up UMKHONTO WE SIZWE (MK)
South Africa leaves British COMMONWEALTH
and becomes a REPUBLIC

**1962** Mandela arrested
**1964** Rivonia Trial

**Second phase of apartheid (1958–1985)**

**1969** Morogoro ANC Conference
Biko forms South African
Students' Organisation (SASO)

**1976** Soweto school pupils' uprising

**1983** UNITED DEMOCRATIC FRONT (UDF) set up

**1985** Serious rioting in townships;
State of Emergency declared

**State of Emergency (1985–1994)**

**1991** CONVENTION FOR A DEMOCRATIC SOUTH
AFRICA (CODESA) meets for first talks

**1994** First democratic election in South Africa's history won
by ANC; Mandela becomes President

–1948–
–1950–
–1960–
–1970–
–1980–
–1990–
–1994–

**1948** National Party wins election; Dr Malan becomes
Prime Minister
**1949** Prohibition of Mixed Marriages Act
**1950** Population Registration Act
Suppression of COMMUNISM Act
Group Areas Act
**1952** Native Laws (Amendment) Act, Abolition of Passes Act
**1953** Separate Amenities Act
Bantu Education Act
**1958** Verwoerd becomes Prime Minister
**1959** Bantu Self-Government Act

**1965** Verwoerd assassinated; Vorster becomes Prime Minister

**1975** Portuguese governments in Angola and Mozambique
overthrown
**1976** Transkei becomes first Bantustan to gain 'independence'
**1977** Biko killed by South African police
**1978** P.W. Botha becomes Prime Minister

**1980** Black government takes over in Zimbabwe

**1984** Botha becomes President under new CONSTITUTION

**1989** De Klerk becomes President
**1990** Mandela released
Violence between ANC and INKATHA supporters

**S**OURCE 3 A timeline of events in South Africa between 1948 and 1994

# chapter 1

# WHY IS HISTORY IMPORTANT TO SOUTH AFRICANS?

## '*The greatest masterpiece of the centuries': how did the Afrikaners tell their history?*

### ■ TALKING POINTS

Human beings like to belong. They like to feel they are members of a particular group or nation. They describe what their group is like according to a number of factors, such as:

- their skin colour
- their language
- their way of life
- their religious beliefs
- their habits and customs
- the stage of technological development they have reached
- their attitude to other groups
- their history – or, at least, their beliefs about their history.

1. What group – or groups – do you feel you belong to?
2. Which of the factors above is important to the group – or groups – you belong to?
3. What is the history of the group – or groups – you belong to?
4. Is this history important to you?

### ■ ACTIVITY

Afrikaners are white South Africans of Dutch origin. You are going to read how an Afrikaner might have told the first 200 years of his people's history. As you do so, think about how this history led Afrikaners to believe these five things about themselves.

1. 'We have a superior civilisation to any other peoples in South Africa.'
2. 'We settled most of South Africa, which was empty before we came.'
3. 'The British are hypocrites, and our enemies.'
4. 'We built up this country.'
5. 'We have been chosen by God to rule in South Africa.'

**1. First settlers**
European ships on their way to East Africa, India or the East Indies had sailed round the Cape of Good Hope since the late fifteenth century. Some sailors had landed for supplies of fresh water, but we Dutch were the first white people actually to settle at the Cape. That was in 1652, and the settlers were led by Jan van Riebeck.

**2. First encounters with Africans**
We began to farm the land – some people call us 'Boers', which means 'farmers'. The only Africans living around the Cape were called Khoi. They sometimes complained that our farms disrupted their grazing grounds, but we easily drove them off. We had guns; they didn't. Those who didn't get killed, or die, became our servants. We introduced simple laws to keep control of these people: they had to carry a pass to show who they were and why they were there.

**3. The Trekboers**
Gradually we began to move away from the coast. We made what we called 'treks': journeys inland, with all our belongings in a cart pulled by oxen. There seemed to be unlimited space: the land was not used. We could claim as much land as we wanted. We liked to live where we could not see another house in any direction. We paid no taxes, had no police, did not vote, made our own laws.

SOURCE 1 Daniel Malan became Prime Minister of South Africa in 1948 and began to introduce apartheid. He saw the events of Afrikaner history as clear evidence that God favoured his people

66 *Our History is the greatest masterpiece of the centuries. We hold this nationhood as our due, as it was given us by the Architect of the Universe. His aim was the formation of a new nation among the nations of the earth. The last 100 years have witnessed a miracle behind which must lie a divine plan. Indeed, the History of the Afrikaner reveals a will and a determination which makes one feel that Afrikanerdom is not the work of men but the creation of God.* 99

## ■ TALKING POINT

### An inside story

The main picture on this spread is what we call 'an artist's reconstruction'. A lot of history books include these now. They convey a lot of historical information. It is important to get them right. If they are wrong you may get a wrong impression of history. So the artist doesn't just make it up. The artist uses references from the past. In this case we sent the artist the picture at the top which was painted in the early nineteenth century. Compare the two.

■ What changes has the artist made?
■ Why do you think he/she has made them?
■ Do you think these changes matter? Explain your reasons.
■ Were we right to use an artist's drawing rather than the original painting here?

### 4. White superiority
Our success proves to us that God is with us. Our technology is better; our God is better; therefore white people are superior to blacks.

### 6. Encounters with black Africans
As we went inland, further east, we began to meet up with black Africans, cattle herders like us. There was plenty of room for us all, but if it came to a fight the gun and the Bible were always on our side.

### 7. British rule
Then the British came. They began to settle from 1795 and took over the government of the Cape in 1806. They were in the middle of their INDUSTRIAL REVOLUTION. They had far greater resources and manpower. They had a huge empire. They brought their own laws and customs, a different version of Christianity, and the English language. So 'the world's most isolated whites' met 'the world's most technologically advanced whites'.
  The British had a different attitude to relations between blacks and whites. Most of them believed, like us, that white people were superior. But they didn't like to say so in so many words. We thought they were hypocrites. Some British actually believed in racial equality, often on religious grounds: that God created all human beings. In 1807 Britain banned the slave trade, in 1828 they abolished our pass laws and in 1834 slavery was abolished throughout the British Empire – including South Africa.

### 5. The Afrikaans language
By the mid-eighteenth century we had lost touch with Europe. We lived one or two months' journey by ox-wagon from Cape Town, then four months by sea from Holland. We developed our own language – Afrikaans, a kind of Dutch, mixed with African and other words. We have been called 'the world's most isolated whites'.

SOURCE 2 A Trekboer in the main room (*voorhuis*) of his house, with his family and servants. His word was law. The speech bubbles contain his version of the Afrikaner history

### 8. The Great Trek

This is the greatest event in our history. In 1836 a group of us Boers set out with our ox-wagons, our cattle, our families and our black slaves and servants to get away from the British. We were fed up with British rule: obeying their laws; paying their taxes; their government officials interfering in our lives. The last straw was the abolition of slavery in 1834. One Boer described this as 'contrary to the laws of God and the natural differences of race and religion'. We were just looking for somewhere where we could live our lives in peace in the way we wanted to.

**SOURCE 3** Wouter Schouten, a Dutch settler, writing in 1665

*" Although descended from our Father Adam, the Khoi have so little of humanity that truly they are no more reasonable than the unreasonable beasts, having no knowledge of God. Miserable folk, how lamentable is your pitiable condition! And, Oh Christians, how blessed is ours! "*

### 9. The Battle of Blood River

The journey was hard. Often our ox-wagons had to struggle over mountain ranges no white people had ever crossed before. Our leader was Piet Retief, but in 1838 he was killed in a battle with Zulu soldiers. As the Zulus prepared to attack us again, our new leader, Andreas Pretorius, organised our wagons into a circle – we call it a laager. There were only 500 of us and 10,000 Zulu warriors outside.

As we got ready to face them, we made a vow to God that if we survived we would always remember the day with thanks. In fact we drove the Zulus off, killing more than 3,000 of them. Not one Boer was killed. This surely was a sign from God that He was on our side. We call this victory the Battle of Blood River.

**SOURCE 4** A painting of wagons on the Great Trek

**SOURCE 5** A British observer describes a Zulu attack

❝ Here they come, black as hell and thick as grass. They wear ear-flaps of green monkey-skin, otterskin headbands, high ostrich plumes. They advance at a trot, hissing and rattling their spears against their shields. ❞

**SOURCE 6** The account of the vow, written in 1876, by Sarel Cilliers, who was at Blood River and later became a minister in the Dutch Reformed Church

❝ I took my place on a guncarriage. My words were these: 'My brethren and my fellow-countrymen, at this moment we stand before the holy God of Heaven and earth to make a promise if He will be with us and protect us and deliver the enemy into our hands ... that we shall preserve the day and the date as an anniversary in each year.' ❞

**SOURCE 7** A painting of the Boer *laager*, or circle of wagons, at the Battle of Blood River. In this situation, because of the cliff, the laager was shaped like a 'D' not as a circle

**10. New republics**
The land we found was mainly empty, so we claimed it for ourselves. We set up two independent Boer republics, the South African Republic (later called the Transvaal) in 1852 and the Orange Free State in 1854.

1. How has the artist of Source 4 emphasised the difficulties the Boers had to overcome on the Great Trek?
2. Why do you think it has been drawn in this way?
3. Look at Source 6. Andreas Pretorius, writing his own account of the Battle of Blood River in 1838, did not mention this vow. Most Afrikaner versions of the story say that this event did take place. Does this prove that what people believe about history is more important than what actually happened?

## ■ TASK

1. What kind of people do these Afrikaners seem to be?

> brave; proud; caring; confident; arrogant; narrow-minded; selfish

Choose three of the words from the box above and explain why you have chosen them, using examples from the history told here.

2. Choose three more words of your own and explain your choice.
3. Look back to the list of ways people belong in the Talking Point on page 10. Which of these factors were important to the Afrikaners?
4. The events described on pages 10–13 are all true, but the story may not be the whole truth. What questions would you want to ask about this story before deciding whether it is an accurate account?

# Who are the South Africans?

ON PAGES 10–13 YOU read the story of the Afrikaners. But there are many other peoples who live in South Africa. They have their histories too. Nelson Mandela, who was democratically elected President of South Africa in 1994, and Desmond Tutu, Archbishop of Cape Town and Nobel Peace Prize-winner, both talk of the South Africans as '**a rainbow people**'. This crowd shows just some of them.

RAINBOW

My ancestors were Portuguese. They came to Africa in the sixteenth century but I moved to South Africa in 1975.

My ancestors came here between about AD300 and AD1000. I speak the Pedi language.

My ancestors were born from white Dutch fathers and African slave mothers in 1700.

My parents were Hungarian. They moved here in 1956.

My grandparents were Jews. They came here in 1926.

My ancestors were brought here from India to work on sugar plantations in 1865.

My ancestors came here between about AD300 and AD1000. I speak the Zulu language.

# PEOPLE

My ancestors were British. They came here in 1822.

My ancestors came here as sailors working on ships from India in 1750.

My ancestors came here between about AD300 and AD1000. I speak the Tswana language.

My ancestors were the Khoi people. We came here 3,000 years ago.

My ancestors came here between about AD300 and AD1000. I speak the XHOSA language.

My ancestors were French. They came here in 1685.

My ancestors were Dutch. They came here in 1652.

My ancestors came here between about AD300 and AD1000. I speak the Sotho language.

Clearly lots of different groups of people have come to live in South Africa and this book is mainly about relations between them in the years 1948 to 1994. In 1946 the government divided them into just four groups:

■ blacks (69 per cent)
■ whites (21 per cent)
■ Coloureds (8 per cent)
■ Asians (2 per cent).

## ■ TASK

1. Everybody has a history. One part of this history is 'How long have we been here?' Use a copy of the chart below to show when each of the peoples on the page opposite arrived in South Africa.

| Date of arrival | Peoples who arrived |
|---|---|
| Before 1000BC | |
| After AD1000 | |
| Before 1700 | |
| 1700–1900 | |
| After 1900 | |

2. There now follow the stories of some of the other peoples of South Africa. As you read through them, think about the Afrikaners' story on pages 10–13 and whether these other stories support or contradict it.

# Who are the black people of South Africa?

## 1. The San and the Khoi

The original inhabitants of what we now call South Africa were living in the Cape area 3,000 years ago. There were two groups: the **San** (called 'bushmen' by whites), who were hunter-gatherers, and the **Khoi** (called 'Hottentots' by whites from their language which includes clicking sounds). The Khoi were herders of goats and sheep.

The San were hunted down by whites and are now extinct in South Africa. There was a serious Khoi uprising from 1799 to 1803, but most fell victim to white diseases and became little more than slaves on white farms.

## 2. Black Africans

Between about AD300 and AD1000, black people from further north in Africa arrived in the east and north of South Africa. They were more technologically advanced than the San and Khoi, with the ability to make iron tools, gold jewellery, pottery and other items. They belonged to different ETHNIC GROUPS with different languages, but there was a network of trading links between them across Africa. They herded cattle and goats, but also grew crops. They had enough to live on. The land was owned collectively, rather than by individuals. In fact, they believed that the land, like the air, could not be parcelled up and owned.

Life in their villages, or *kraals*, was governed by complex rules of behaviour. There were clearly defined roles for men and women: women grew crops, made pottery and looked after the children; men hunted and looked after the herds of animals. They had a word, *ubuntu*, which means that an individual is important within the group.

There were perhaps 3.5 million black South Africans in 1900.

It wasn't necessarily an idyllic life: there were fierce wars between rival groups. Rules could be harsh. Drought produced famines in which many died. Sources 2–5 describe life in black African villages before they were much influenced by contact with whites.

**SOURCE 1** San hunters in about 1830

**SOURCE 2** A Matabele *kraal*, from a painting by a white artist, 1836

**SOURCE 3** A nineteenth-century photograph of a Xhosa woman and child from Cape Colony

**SOURCE 4** In 1686 a Dutch ship was wrecked on the coast and the survivors were looked after in a Xhosa village for three years. One survivor recorded his impressions

*It would be impossible to buy any slaves there, for they would not part with their children, loving one another with a most remarkable strength of affection ... They are very civil, polite and talkative, saluting each other, male or female, young or old, whenever they meet, asking where you are from, where you are going, what is your news ... they have in every village a house of entertainment for travellers, where they are not only lodged but fed also.*

**SOURCE 5** A German called Lichtenstein travelled among several villages in 1803 and wrote

*The chief is absolute sovereign, yet there is a power to balance his in the people; he governs only as long as they choose to obey.*

1. Look at Sources 1–5. How useful are these sources as evidence of the lives of black people in southern Africa before contact with whites?
2. What impression of black African life do they give? Select evidence to support your view.
3. Does this view of the black African way of life support the Afrikaner view that they were more civilised than the black Africans?

## Changes in the early 1800s

In the early 1800s there was a series of upheavals among the black peoples of southern Africa. Historians are unsure about the causes. One was the rise of a strong military Zulu kingdom, led by Shaka from 1816–28. Shaka's attacks on other peoples caused chaos over a huge area of southern Africa.

But there were other reasons for these upheavals: demand for slaves in East Africa and South Africa was putting pressure on the traditional way of life. Settlers moving into the area were making it difficult for some people to stay on their lands. There may well have been environmental factors too, for example drought and soil exhaustion, causing mass movements of people.

Some languages call these upheavals MFECANE, which means 'crushing'; others call them DIFAQANE, which means 'forced migration'. Together, the two words sum up the results: governments overthrown, new ones forming, people on the move, many of them starving, and the abandonment of normal settled patterns of living.

## Two views of black history

**SOURCE 6** In south-eastern Africa is a large ruined city, called Zimbabwe, built by black Africans, probably in the fourteenth century. A white South African historian, M. Marshall, writing in 1934 said

*There are no natives today living in South Africa who could have erected such monumental structures. The blacks possess nothing but little huts made of wood and boughs.*

**SOURCE 7** In his biography *No Easy Walk to Freedom*, published in 1965, Nelson Mandela, born in 1918, recalled his childhood

*Then our people lived peacefully, under the democratic rule of their kings and of their councillors, and moved freely and confidently up and down the country without let or hindrance. Then the country was ours ... we occupied the land, the forests, the rivers; we extracted the mineral wealth beneath the soil and all the riches of this beautiful country. We set up and operated our own government, we controlled our own armies and organised our own trade and commerce.*

Read Sources 6 and 7. They give a white and a black view of the past history and achievements of black Africans.

4. Why did the author of Source 6 want to prove that blacks could not have built Zimbabwe?
5. What view of his own past does Nelson Mandela give in Source 7?
6. How accurate do you think it is?
7. Why was it important to him to describe his past in this way?

*17*

# Who are the white people of South Africa?

### 1. The Dutch

You have already read about the arrival of the Dutch settlers in 1652 (see page 10). Their leader, Jan van Riebeck, was an educated man, but many settlers were tough, poorly educated ex-soldiers. Their treatment of the San and Khoi peoples of the Cape area was often brutal. When the Africans complained that the Dutch settlers were creating farms on their traditional grazing lands many were simply hunted and shot.

The Dutch settlers were joined by other Europeans: Germans, Scandinavians and, in the 1680s, French Protestant refugees.

**S**OURCE 8  This painting by a white artist shows Khoi people, who have taken cattle, being hunted by whites

**S**OURCE 9  An eighteenth-century 'Dutch-style' house in the Cape area

### Slaves

Like European colonists all over the world, the Dutch settlers had slaves. They enslaved the San and Khoi, but also brought in slaves from other parts of the Dutch empire: Sri Lanka and Indonesia.

As in other parts of the world, slaves were kept in their places by vicious punishments: whipping and branding. From the 1760s slaves had to have a 'pass' to show who owned them. This was the beginning of the system which caused so much grief to black South Africans in the twentieth century.

Some of the enslaved people were Muslim. They bought their freedom and used their skills as carpenters, tailors and stonemasons to make a living. They built most of the typical 'Dutch-style' Cape houses of the seventeenth and eighteenth centuries. They established a Muslim community in Cape Town, with their own mosque and imam. With the Muslim respect for learning, they were the most literate community in the country: the first book in the Afrikaans language was written by a Muslim. They were fierce in defence of their rights and religious freedoms.

You have read, too, about the 'Trekboers' who moved inland with their cattle in the eighteenth century. The land was not, in fact, 'empty': it was used as grazing ground by black Africans. They presented tougher resistance to the Boers than the San and Khoi of the Cape had done. The first wars between whites and Xhosas took place in 1779. Nor did these Africans fall victim to European diseases, as the San and Khoi did.

8.  Holland is a small country and land is scarce. What new opportunities did Dutch settlers in Africa have which were not open to them back home?

### Cape Coloureds

Most whites arriving in the Dutch colony in the seventeenth and eighteenth centuries were single men. Despite their racial views about black peoples, they had sexual relations with them. The children produced were called COLOUREDS. They spoke Afrikaans and worked as servants and labourers. Many worked in the vineyards, where it was customary to pay part of their wages in wine, with the result that alcoholism was common.

## 2. The British

By the late eighteenth century Britain's Industrial Revolution was well under way and the British Empire in India was growing. A glance at the map showed the British that Cape Colony could be important to securing their route to India. The first British occupation took place in 1795 and it became a British possession in 1806.

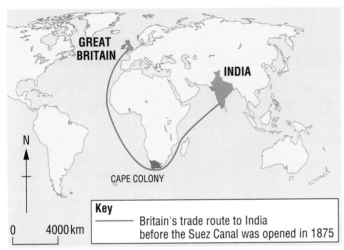

**Key**
—— Britain's trade route to India before the Suez Canal was opened in 1875

GREAT BRITAIN
INDIA
CAPE COLONY
N
0   4000 km

**SOURCE 10** A map showing the position of the Cape on the route to India

The impact of British rule on the Boers from 1806 was two-sided. Many Boers benefited from links with the British trading empire and became prosperous sheep farmers. There is evidence that many of those who set out on the Great Trek, were poorer farmers, unable to benefit from British connections. Certainly Piet Retief was deeply in debt and, for him and those like him, the Great Trek was a way of making a clean start. Only about 15,000 Boers left the Cape between 1834 and 1850.

Nor did they find 'empty' land. Some areas may well have been underpopulated as a result of the *difaqane/mfecane*, but that was only temporary. Black settlers soon moved into the land claimed by the trekkers and farmed alongside them. Some trekkers tried to come to an arrangement with Xhosa chiefs to settle on their lands by agreement. In other places trekkers were driven out by black settlers.

**SOURCE 11** The British tried to create settlements in the eastern Cape, at Grahamstown and Port Elizabeth. The area was described in glowing terms by Lord Charles Somerset

66 *The place resembles a succession of parks, in which, upon a verdant [green] carpet, Nature has planted in endless variety. The soil is well-adapted for cultivation.* 99

Somerset's glowing description was quite wrong. The first 120 settlers, in 1820, had to deal with drought, locusts and crop diseases. The plan, to grow crops in market gardens, was ill thought out: the nearest market for fresh food was 900 km to the west in Cape Town. By 1823 only a third of the original settlers were left. The survivors turned to business or trade – or began to move inland.

This brought them into conflict with the black Africans of the interior. The British fought almost continuous frontier wars against the Xhosa and other peoples from 1819 to 1853. In the end, with horses, guns and trained soldiers, the British were bound to win. A new British colony in Natal was founded in 1843. At first the British agreed that the Zulus should have the land to the north, but later they decided to seize Zulu lands. Although Chief Cetshwayo inflicted a famous crushing defeat on the British at Isandhlwana in 1879, the Zulus were broken by 1897.

### Indians

British settlers in Natal found that sugar-cane grew well there, but they needed workers for the plantations. From 1860 to 1911 a total of 152,000 Indian labourers were brought to South Africa. When their contracts were over, about half of them decided to stay, so forming the ancestors of the South African Indian community.

## ■ TASK

1. You have now read the Afrikaners' own view of their history alongside the stories of some of the other groups in South Africa. Can you find examples of:
   a) ways in which the Afrikaners' story is not quite accurate?
   b) ways in which the Afrikaners' story is not quite complete?
   c) ways in which the Afrikaners' story is correct?
2. Is it important to try to establish the whole and exact truth about history?
3. Why is history important to the different groups of people in the 'rainbow nation' of South Africa?
4. Can you think of other parts of the world today where history is important to a group of people?

As you read through this book, think about which is more important: history, or what people believe about their history.

# How did the South African War affect relations between the Boers and the British?

THE BOERS WHO went on the Great Trek did so in order to be left alone in peace. They were not to be left alone for long. Diamonds were discovered in Kimberley, in the Orange Free State, in 1867. People flocked to the mine from all over the world. Within ten years diamonds worth £60 million had been found and Kimberley was a bustling town of 30,000 people, second only to Cape Town in size. In 1886, gold was discovered near Johannesburg. By the beginning of the twentieth century Johannesburg had a population of nearly 250,000 people and was by far the biggest city in southern Africa. The British government of Cape Colony and Natal looked enviously at the wealth of the diamond and gold mines in the Boer republics.

The last quarter of the nineteenth century was the time of greatest British imperial expansion. One of the keenest imperialists was Cecil Rhodes, an Englishman who had come to South Africa aged 18 in 1871. He had become a diamond and gold mine-owner and was Prime Minister of the Cape. He had plans for British expansion all the way up the east side of Africa, 'from the Cape to Cairo'. Many of the miners and mine-owners were British and supported the idea of a British take-over. War between the British and the Boers seemed likely sooner or later.

A British attack on Transvaal in 1881 was defeated, but in 1899 the Boer War (as it was known in Britain) began. At first the Boers, with their better knowledge of the country and skills as marksmen, hunters and horsemen, did well, but the British had more men, money and equipment with which to fight, and by 1900 organised Boer forces were defeated. However, groups of

SOURCE 1 A cartoon of Cecil Rhodes astride Africa from the Cape to Cairo

Boers kept on fighting a GUERRILLA war against the occupying British army for another two years.

The British response was to make it impossible for the bands of Boer guerrillas to survive in the countryside. They burnt the farmhouses and moved the women and children into CONCENTRATION CAMPS. Here, in confined conditions, without proper food, hygiene and medicine, 28,000 of them died. This was 25 per cent of the Boer population. The Boers surrendered in 1902 and peace was made at Vereeniging.

To the bitterness of the Boers over the deaths of women and children in the concentration camps was now added another grievance: language. Lord Milner, British High Commissioner in South Africa, decided that now that the Boers were part of the British Empire, they had to learn English. English was now used in schools and children could be punished for speaking Afrikaans.

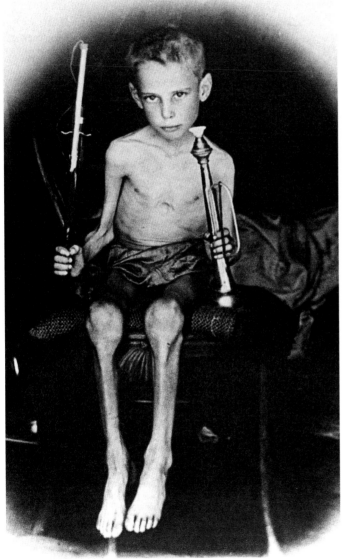

**S**OURCE 2  A malnourished Boer child in a British concentration camp

**S**OURCE 3  Lord Milner sets out his intentions for the new South Africa

*66 2/5 Boers and 3/5 British – peace, progress and fusion; 3/5 Boers and 2/5 British – stagnation and eternal discord. 99*

**S**OURCE 4  An Afrikaner describes the attempt to make him speak English

*66 If you were caught speaking Afrikaans, you had to carry a placard round your neck bearing the words 'must not speak Dutch'. When the bell went for school to end the last boy with what was called the Dutch Mark had to write out one thousand times 'I must speak English at school.' 99*

## Boer War or South African War?

Many historians now call this war the South African War. They point out that it was not an all-white affair: something like 100,000 black people took part. They were mainly scouts, runners or baggage-carriers, but 10,000 blacks were armed. They fought on both sides, but mainly for the British. Some idea of attitudes to the races can be seen in Sources 5 and 6 from the siege of Mafeking in 1899.

**S**OURCE 5  An extract from a letter written by the Boer commander Cronje to the British commander in Mafeking, Baden-Powell, when he learnt that the British had armed black soldiers

*66 It is understood you have armed the natives. In this you have committed an enormous act of wickedness. Reconsider the matter, even if it should cost you the loss of Mafeking – disarm your blacks and thereby act the part of a white man in a white man's war. 99*

**S**OURCE 6  A note from Baden-Powell's diary. He eventually forced blacks out of the town, and many of them then died of starvation

*66 April 20ᵗʰ: Meat and meal stocks will last until June 12ᵗʰ. But by forcing natives away from Mafeking, we can get their share of horseflesh for whites. 99*

1.  What similarities are there between the attitudes of the two enemies towards black people?

## ■ TASK

1.  Explain in your own words what Lord Milner means in Source 3.
2.  What does this source tell you about British plans for their colony in South Africa?
3.  List the grievances the Boers had against the British as a result of the South African War.

# chapter 2

# WAS SOUTH AFRICA RACIALLY SEGREGATED IN 1948?

THE CORE OF this book begins in 1948, when a new government took over in South Africa, determined to put into practice a policy called 'apartheid', which means separateness. They planned, as you will see in Chapter 4, to separate black and white South Africans as much as possible. But separation, or SEGREGATION, of black and white people did not begin in 1948. This chapter looks at the extent to which South Africa was racially segregated before apartheid began, and why.

You have already seen, in Chapter 1, that the white rulers of South Africa, Dutch and British, treated black people unequally. They fought them, took their land, forced them to work, enslaved them and regarded them as inferior human beings. However, separation of the races had not yet taken place.

- South Africa was still an agricultural country, with black and white farmers, often on neighbouring farms.
- Rich whites had black servants, but poor whites and blacks lived and worked alongside one another.
- After the problems of the *difaqane* (see page 17), having lost wars against white rule, black Africans had begun to settle down as small farmers. They were good at it: they knew the land and the climate. Men and women worked on the land together. In areas near to towns they sold their produce to the growing urban population.

At the end of the nineteenth century the discovery of diamonds and gold – usually called the 'Mining Revolution' – changed South Africa and the lives of its people utterly.

# How did the Mining Revolution increase racial segregation?

## ■ TASK

The Mining Revolution made South Africa rich, but it totally changed the lives of black Africans. As you read about how minework became organised, look for evidence of:

- how different miners' lives were from their lives back in their home villages
- how the lives of their relatives were changed by minework
- how racial segregation became part of the mining industry in South Africa.

SOURCE 1 The 'Big Hole' at Kimberley, in the Orange Free State, where diamonds were discovered in 1867. It is the biggest man-made hole in the world. This picture was taken 12 months after the start of the digging. PROSPECTORS dug for diamonds in their tiny claims – less than two metres square – and carried the soil out on hundreds of lines to the edge of the 'hole'. But as the mine grew deeper they needed pumps and other equipment. Only those with money could keep going and rich businessmen bought out individual miners

MINING DIAMONDS WAS an expensive business but mining gold cost even more. There was plenty of gold, but it was very deep, about 1 km down. It was also of poor quality: two tonnes of ore produced only 21 grams of gold. This meant that huge investments had to be made in equipment, labour and time spent digging. It was estimated that it cost 60 million RAND just to start a mine, before any gold had been extracted.

This meant that the mine-owners (the 'Randlords', as they were called) had a problem. The mines were tremendously expensive to set up and operate; the price of gold was fixed internationally.

- How could the mine-owners increase their profits?
  **Answer:** by hiring cheap labour.
- And where could they find cheap labour?
  **Answer:** from the black Africans in the villages.

But to bring workers and their families to Johannesburg would involve huge, expensive housing schemes. They would have to pay high enough wages to keep the miner and his family alive. And the blacks didn't want to come anyway.

So the mine-owners developed the MIGRANT LABOUR SYSTEM.

## The migrant labour system

The system worked like this.

### The attraction

1. Agents were sent out into the countryside to attract young, unmarried men to work in the mines.

2. At first it seemed quite a good offer: the young man signed a contract to work for a few months.

3. He went to the Rand, where he was housed in a compound with other men from his ethnic group.

4. His contract done, he returned home. He needed cash to pay the parents of the girl he wanted to marry the 'bride-price'.

5. Cash was also useful because some black Africans had begun to abandon their SUBSISTENCE lifestyle and wanted to buy manufactured goods.

### The reality

1. Mine-owners paid low wages because they were providing housing and food.

2. They also paid low wages because the miners' families were back home living off the land.

3. The work was hard: miners worked 1 km underground, in tough, dangerous conditions.

4. They were housed in squalid compound blocks.

5. They were harshly treated by their overseers.

**SOURCE 2** Gold was discovered on the Witwatersrand (usually called 'the Rand') near Johannesburg in 1886. This picture was taken in 1888

Black workers were not willing to come in enough numbers to satisfy the mine-owners' needs. Mine-owners found they had to pay higher wages than they wanted to. Agents were sent all over Africa looking for workers, bringing them hundreds of kilometres from the Portuguese colony of Mozambique and British colonies in central Africa.

## Government help

The mine-owners turned to the government for help. The Boer governments of the Orange Free State and Transvaal found themselves in a strange position. The farmers who made up their population were not rich and not keen on paying their taxes. In 1884 the Transvaal was almost bankrupt. Then came this enormous flood of money and people into their farmers' republic. By 1887 the Transvaal had an income of 3 million rand. But the mine-owners wanted something in return for their money. They made the government pass a law to introduce a Hut Tax. This meant that every hut, every family, had to pay 1 rand each year in tax. But most blacks in rural areas still did not use money – when they needed goods, they exchanged some of their own goods in payment. How could they get cash? By sending someone to work in the mines, naturally.

**SOURCE 5** Men leaving their homes to go to work in the Kimberley diamond mines

**SOURCE 3** This picture shows Johannesburg around 1910. By 1913 the Rand was supplying 40 per cent of the world's gold

**SOURCE 4** An appeal by the President of the Chamber of Mines to the government in 1912

66 *We must have labour. The mining industry without labour is as bricks would be without straw or to imagine you could get milk without a cow ... The native cares nothing if industries pine for want of labour when his crops and home-brewed drink are plentiful.* 99

**SOURCE 6** This sign was put up in Lesotho in 1906

66 *NOTICE TO STRONG BOYS.*
*I wish to make it publicly known that I have stopped flogging at Picaninny Kimberley Compound. Today is your time to earn money. Wages are from 3 shillings to 10 shillings a day, according to your strength. I shall pay Hut Tax for you and railway fare to Picaninny Kimberley. Now, my friends, it is time for you to come. The cattle have udders, come and milk them.* 99

S OURCE 7  Women and children were left to look after the home and the land while the men worked away

1. What does the author of Source 4 find wrong with the situation he is describing?
2. What does Source 6 tell you about the migrant labour system?
3. What were the benefits of the migrant labour system for the mine-owners?
4. The mine-owners were rich and powerful. Why did they need the government to do something for them?
5. In what way was the government's help essential in getting what the mine-owners wanted?

## Life for the miners

Life for the miners was grim. They lived in compounds which were cold, crowded and unhealthy. Their work underground was hard, dusty, noisy and dangerous. They were driven by the whips of the white supervisors. Gradually the length of their contracts was increased from six months to eight or nine months.

To stop the miners running away, each miner had to carry a passbook, showing who he was and where he worked. Any black male could be stopped by the police and asked for his pass at any time.

It was difficult to organise mineworkers into unions to fight for better conditions: they were not allowed to leave their compounds, they spoke different languages, and strikes were fiercely crushed by their employers.

S OURCE 8  J.H. Johns, in a speech to mine managers in 1894, justified conditions in the compounds

66 *In their own kraals, natives live in a more or less backward state of civilisation, and there is, in my opinion, a danger that we may be going too far in our efforts to make them comfortable and I think that the natives far prefer those compounds which are not too well-ventilated and airy.* 99

S OURCE 9  In 1918 a short-lived union called the Industrial Workers of South Africa called on workers to see that ethnic differences were becoming irrelevant

66 *There is only one way to freedom, black workers: unite as workers, unite! Forget the things that divide you. Let there be no longer any talk of Basuto, Zulu, or Shangaan. You are all labourers: Let labour be your common bond!* 99

S OURCE 10  A striker at the Knights Deep Mine complained in 1920

66 *The white man goes below, does no work and gets big money. The African gets all the gold out of the ground and gets very little money. How is that fair?* 99

## ■ TASK

1. In what ways did the growth of the mining industry in South Africa lead to a worsening of the position of black Africans?
2. Make a list of the grievances black mineworkers had.
3. Why was it so difficult for them to do anything about these grievances?

## ■ ACTIVITY

Working in pairs, look at the Universal Declaration of Human Rights on pages 4–5. Discuss which of the rights were broken by the migrant labour system.

# How did white rule before 1948 affect black South Africans?

THE BRITISH HAD said that one reason why they were fighting the Boers in the South African War was to protect the rights of black people. Black South Africans welcomed the British victory in 1902. They were to be sorely disappointed.

South Africa was now part of the British Empire and decisions were taken in London or by the British High Commissioner in South Africa. Yet the Union of South Africa, formed in 1910, set up a government elected almost entirely by whites. A few thousand better-off Coloureds in the Cape still had the right to vote, but even they lost this right in 1936. Africans and Indians had no voting rights at all. A deputation of South Africans of mixed races went to London in 1909, while union was being discussed, to plead for voting rights for all. No one in London took any notice. Why did the British do this?

Some British felt guilty about the war against the Boers. Furthermore, South Africa's tremendous wealth was now in the British Empire. The British decided to hold out the olive branch to their ex-enemies to keep the country united. The 'alliance of gold and maize', that is, the business interests of the mine-owners and the big farmers, overcame the principles the British had proclaimed as their reason for fighting the war.

In the First World War many black Africans fought for Britain; 5,635 of them died. Another deputation went to Britain in 1919 to ask for an improvement in their civil rights, but they were again ignored.

**SOURCE 1** The South African deputation to Britain, 1909. There were blacks, Coloureds, and one white MP. They went to try to persuade the British government to introduce full democratic rights for all South Africans

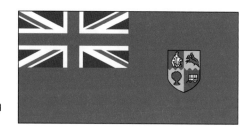

**SOURCE 2** The Union Flag of South Africa, 1910

## ■ TASK

Not being able to vote and having no say in government decisions left black South Africans in a very weak position. What happened to them shows just how important the vote is in any society. We are going to look at how they lost out in three important areas: **land**, **housing** and **jobs**. As you work through this investigation, complete a copy of the table below.

|  | Land | Housing | Jobs |
|---|---|---|---|
| How did the law separate blacks and whites? |  |  |  |
| In what ways were they treated separately? |  |  |  |
| In what ways were they treated unequally? |  |  |  |
| Was South Africa already segregated in this area by 1948? |  |  |  |

# Land

At the beginning of the twentieth century, seven out of eight black South Africans lived in rural areas. Many were successful small farmers. The growth of towns and cities and the rising population meant that there was a good market for the food they produced. Black Africans often farmed more successfully than Afrikaners. One reason for this was that they simply had more labour: it was part of the African tradition for women to work on the land, while Afrikaner women did not. Many blacks also farmed as share-croppers, a system in which the share-cropper gave part of his crop (usually half) to the white landowners in return for the land he used.

**SOURCE 5** A successful farmstead run by black Africans

**SOURCE 3** A comment made by a British visitor to South Africa in 1910

*66 Man for man, the kaffir [a white term for black Africans] is a better farmer than the European; more careful of their animals, cultivating a larger area of land, working themselves more industriously. 99*

**SOURCE 4** An old Sotho woman, Nkono Mma-Pooe, was recorded in 1983 talking about her early life. Here, she describes her husband, Naphthali, a share-cropper

*66 Naphthali was a hard worker. Indeed he worked very hard in his fields. He produced a lot from the soil. Hundreds of bags [of produce], half of which he gave to Theuns [the farmer] who in turn sold them and got a lot of money from the labour to which he had contributed nothing. 99*

Africans were very reluctant to give up farming, but the mine-owners and farmers wanted their labour, in the mines and on the land. So the 'alliance of gold and maize' got the white government to pass the Natives Land Act of 1913. According to this Act:

- blacks could not own or rent land except in the black RESERVATIONS. These made up only 7 per cent of the land, although the area was extended to 13 per cent by the 1936 Natives Land Act (see Source 6). They were far away from towns and cities
- share-cropping was banned. Blacks could only occupy white-owned land if they worked for the farmer.

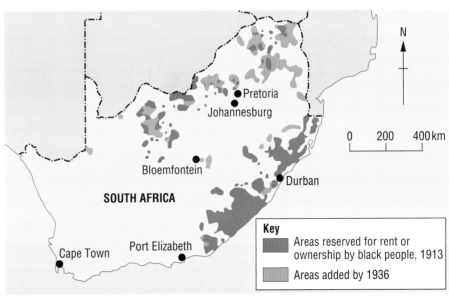

**SOURCE 6** A map showing land reserved for black ownership or rent by the Natives Land Acts of 1913 and 1936

Sol Plaatje, a black writer, bicycled all over the country finding out about the effects of the 1913 Land Act. In his book *Native Life in South Africa*, published in 1916, he described the hardship he had seen. He told the story of Kgobadi, a black share-cropper. Before the Act, Kgobadi made £100 a year after giving half his crop to the farmer. When the Act was brought in he was told he could only stay if he handed over his oxen and if he and his wife worked full time for the farmer for a joint wage of £18 a year. He refused and was given until nightfall to leave. He and his family set off on the road.

### ■ ACTIVITY

1. Look at Sources 4 and 6. What do you think happened to Naphthali after the 1913 Natives Land Act was passed? Write another episode in his story, describing the impact of the Act on him and his family.
2. What do you think happened to Kgobadi? Write another episode in his story, describing him ending up in a city, looking for work.
3. Do you think the Act affected Naphthali and Kgobadi in similar ways?

### ■ TASK 1

1. What was the condition of black farmers before the 1913 Natives Land Act?
2. How did the Act affect them?
3. How did the Act affect white farmers?
4. What do you think the long-term effects of the Act on black people might have been?

Now complete the first section of the table on page 26.

**S**OURCE 7  The new township of Meadowlands, outside Johannesburg

**S**OURCE 8  The City Engineer of Johannesburg describes how the cost of building houses at Orlando was kept low. They had two rooms, one door at the front, no doors between rooms, dirt floors and no ceilings

*66 Ceilings were omitted on account of the extra expense entailed as well as to give additional air-space in the buildings. 99*

## Housing

The view of most whites was that Africans were rural people, not suited to urban life. Nevertheless, they wanted black people to come and work in their mines and factories, and as domestic servants. More and more Africans moved into the towns and particularly to those areas where poor white people lived. There was a single but powerful difference between poor whites and poor blacks: the whites had the vote. Politicians had to pay attention to their problems. This was why they decided to segregate housing: so that poor whites could be housed at the expense of blacks.

The government set up the Stallard Commission to look into the situation. The result was the Native (Urban Areas) Act of 1923. This allowed local councils to segregate housing in towns into 'black' and 'white' areas and to build new black townships.

Inside towns, the more desirable areas were allocated for 'whites only' housing. The houses available to Africans were often run-down, older properties and their yards. Town councils demolished black housing in areas declared 'white'. The inhabitants had to move, often many kilometres away, to segregated 'black locations'. Here, cheap new housing was built to very basic standards (see Sources 7 and 8). Africans living in these new townships faced long, tedious and expensive journeys to work.

The Act was not fully enforced everywhere. In some places, like Sophiatown in Johannesburg and District Six in Cape Town, black people owned houses or had secure leases. Blacks and whites lived side by side.

**SOURCE 9** A group of British social workers visited South Africa and wrote about what they saw in the British weekly journal *New Statesman and Nation,* September 1939

66 *Most Africans living in Johannesburg are segregated into separate townships and locations ... For the whole of one township there is only one Medical Officer and one health visitor for the 15,000 residents. Schools are available for only 38 per cent of the African children in Johannesburg.* 99

**SOURCE 10** Naboth Mokgatle, a black activist, describes the demolition of black housing in 1940

66 *One day I witnessed a sight which broke my heart and which I have never been able to forget. Near Marabastad was an African location, Schonplatts. I saw the City Council's workmen brought in to demolish Schonplatts, and as they did so to throw the inhabitants and their belongings out. That drove me into politics. It was the end of Schonplatts. In its place was a football ground and playing field for white children. Schonplatts was a slum, but that was not why it was demolished.* 99

## Passes

The Stallard Commission wanted to restrict the numbers of blacks entering towns and to make their stay temporary. This was done by extending the pass system, which had existed since the eighteenth century in some places. Every black male had to carry a passbook giving his address, employer, wages and other personal details. He could be stopped at any time by the police and required to show it.

1. Why do you think the pass system was so hated by black South Africans?

**SOURCE 12** An extract from a report by the Stallard Commission, 1923

66 *(Africans) should only be permitted within urban areas in so far and for so long as their presence is demanded by the wants of the white population.* 99

## ■ TASK 2

1. What did the law do to create separate housing areas for blacks and whites?
2. In what ways were blacks and whites treated separately?
3. In what ways were they treated unequally?
4. Were South Africans already segregated in housing by 1948?

Use your answers to these questions to complete the second column of the table on page 26.

**SOURCE 11** District Six, an old area of black-owned housing near the centre of Cape Town which was not cleared until the 1970s

## Jobs

There had always been separate jobs for whites and blacks in South Africa. In the mines, for example, whites had supervisors' jobs, while black workers could only be labourers at a much lower rate of pay. Segregation was extended in the decades before 1948.

In the 1920s poor white farmers, called *bywoners*, found themselves unable to make a living. There were droughts and epidemics of disease. More and more of them gave up farming and drifted to the towns. Here, they could only afford the cheapest housing in areas where blacks also lived.

As with housing, the Government passed laws to ensure job segregation too.

■ Industrial Conciliation Act, 1924. This allowed white workers to join trade unions, but barred black workers from doing so.
■ Mines and Works Act, 1926. This restricted a whole range of jobs to whites only. It was called a 'civilised labour policy'. Most famously, jobs on the railways were restricted. Every railway worker, from management to drivers, clerks, wheel-tappers, fitters and labourers, was white. By 1942 it was estimated that one in eleven working white males worked for the South African Railways.

**S**OURCE 13  Poor whites in Johannesburg in the 1930s

**S**OURCE 14  A *bywoner* describes his arrival in Johannesburg

❝ *Man, I felt like a rabbit thrown into a cageful of dogs. Wherever you look there are people. It was a frightening discovery to walk in the streets. I was so far from the open plains of the Orange Free State and to be in Jo'burg was a terrible thing.* ❞

**S**OURCE 15  An extract from a government report of 1914

❝ *The European minority, occupying the position of the dominant race, cannot allow a considerable number of its members to sink into poverty and so to fall below the level of non-European workers.* ❞

**S**OURCE 16  White railway workers in the 1920s

■ **TASK 1**

1. Poor whites and blacks from rural South Africa arrived in the cities in increasing numbers in the 1920s and 1930s. Use Sources 13–19 to make a list of the ways in which their problems and experiences were the same.
2. Compare Sources 11 (see page 29) and 13. Why would the white government be shocked by this comparison?

### The Depression

There was a worldwide ECONOMIC DEPRESSION in the 1930s. Following the Wall Street Crash in the USA in 1929, banks and factories all over the world closed down. The 1930s Depression hit both black and white South Africans hard. The government was shocked to learn that one in five whites was in dire poverty. The situation for blacks was certainly worse, but again the fact that only whites had votes ensured that the whites were helped.

Blacks were sacked from jobs to provide employment for white workers.

Stricter controls were put on the movement of blacks into towns. Life was made very difficult for blacks working there.

White farmers received a guaranteed price for their products.

## How did the government help whites during the Depression?

Job creation schemes were begun, such as road-building.

Low-cost housing was built for whites.

Government-run corporations were set up to boost the electricity industry (ESCOM) and the iron and steel industry (ISCOR). Both of these provided new jobs for whites only.

**SOURCE 17**  How the government helped whites during the Depression

**SOURCE 18**  Naboth Mokgatle describes the effects of the Depression

*66 Nineteen thirty was a year of depression. Many Africans were out of work and could not find any. Some of them were thrown out of their jobs to make room for European workers. Notices appeared in the windows of many places stating that the work done there was only by white labour. 99*

**SOURCE 19**  A black trader trying to make a living in Johannesburg, 1940

### ■ TASK 2

1. What did the law do to separate whites and blacks at work?
2. In what ways were they treated separately?
3. In what ways were they treated unequally?
4. Were South Africans already segregated in employment by 1948?

Use your answers to these questions to complete the final column of the table on page 26.

### ■ ACTIVITY

Working in pairs, look back to the Universal Declaration of Human Rights on pages 4–5. The Declaration was actually produced *after* the events described in this chapter, but which of the rights do you think were likely to have been broken in South Africa before 1948?

# 3 WHY DID THE NATIONALISTS WIN THE 1948 ELECTION?

## Introduction

THE BOERS – OR Afrikaners as they preferred to call themselves since many were no longer farmers – were (and still are) a majority of the whites in South Africa. Yet before 1948 they had never succeeded in forming a real Afrikaner government. So there was a sense of shock and surprise throughout South Africa when the Nationalists won the general election of May 1948. Their majority over the United Party, led by Jan Smuts, was tiny – just five seats – but they now controlled the country. Dr Daniel Malan became Prime Minister and appointed a cabinet made up entirely of Afrikaners.

1. Read Source 1. What does Dr Malan mean by 'us' and by 'like strangers in our own country'?
2. Read Source 2. What was the attitude of Wentzel du Plessis on being elected?
3. Read Sources 3 and 4. What different reactions did these two black resistance leaders have to the Nationalists' election victory?

In their election campaign, the Nationalists had promised to bring in apartheid. They had outlined their plans in the Sauer Report.

■ The blacks would live in reserves, completely separate from the whites. Those with jobs in white areas would be classed as visitors.
■ Coloureds would also have to live separately and would lose what remained of their political rights.
■ Indians would be sent back to India.
■ Whites would rule; blacks would be kept under control.

Because organised black resistance to white rule had been too successful – and the National Party promised to keep the blacks down?

Because of the changes the Second World War had brought about in South Africa – and the National Party promised to reverse them?

Because the National Party knew how to appeal to white voters?

Why did the Nationalists win power?

**SOURCE 1** Dr Malan describes his feelings on becoming Prime Minister in 1948

*66 In the past we felt like strangers in our own country, but today South Africa belongs to us once more. 99*

**SOURCE 2** A comment made later by Wentzel du Plessis, the Nationalist candidate who defeated the outgoing Prime Minister, Jan Smuts

*66 We were feeling the horizon was lifting; the skies were clearing. There was promise in the air and we were going to use that opportunity – which we did. 99*

**SOURCE 3** Govan Mbeki, a leading member of the African National Congress (ANC), describes his reaction at the time

*66 We wake up one morning and we are told that Malan has won the election. And that meant the door was shut in our faces. 99*

**SOURCE 4** The reaction of Oliver Tambo, leader of the ANC Youth League, to the Nationalists' victory

*66 I like this because it is going to give further momentum to the resistance movement. We now know that we have an enemy in power . . . I think that we are going to have a better opportunity of mobilising our people. 99*

# How effective was organised resistance to segregation before 1948?

## ■ TASK

Use a copy of this table to judge the effectiveness of resistance to segregation as you read the next section. In the first column, make a summary of the methods used by each group; in the second column, give each group a mark out of ten for its effectiveness; and explain the reasons for your mark in the last column.

|  | Methods | Mark out of ten for effectiveness | Evidence to support your mark |
|---|---|---|---|
| **1** ANC |  |  |  |
| **2** Anti-pass demonstrations |  |  |  |
| **3** Indian resistance |  |  |  |
| **4** Trade unions |  |  |  |
| **5** Communists |  |  |  |
| **6** Others |  |  |  |

## 1 How effective was the African National Congress?

You have already read about Sol Plaatje (see page 28). As a young man in 1894, he lived in the diamond town of Kimberley. He was black, but with an Afrikaans name. Educated by German missionaries he worked, with other blacks, in the Post Office, on equal terms with whites. He belonged to a small group of educated, Christian Africans from several ethnic backgrounds in the town. They held debates, went to see plays by Shakespeare, played cricket. Through these activities they had some social contact with liberal whites. They were optimistic about British promises to extend a share of political power to some educated and responsible black Africans. When the South African War came, Sol worked for the British, supplying them with information. As we know, he was to be bitterly disappointed in the British and their promises.

### The formation of the African National Congress

Disappointment over the terms of the Treaty of 1902 and the government of the Union of South Africa (see page 26) led groups of educated Africans in different parts of the country to form local protest organisations. Several of them, including Sol Plaatje, began newspapers to publicise their ideas. But even though black Africans were in a huge majority in the country as a whole, educated Africans were a tiny and isolated minority. When they met, they could not even agree on which language to use at first, as they came from different ethnic groups and despised English as the language of their conquerors.

In 1912 members of many of these organisations met together in Bloemfontein and formed the South African Native National Congress (SANNC). Sol Plaatje was its first secretary. It became the African National Congress (ANC) in 1923.

> ### SOURCE 1 The main aim of the SANNC, as set out in 1912
>
> *66 To encourage mutual understanding and to bring together into common action as one political people all tribes or races and by means of combined effort and united political organisation to defend their freedom, rights and privileges. 99*

There is not a straight line of development from Sol Plaatje to Nelson Mandela. The ANC was pretty ineffective for many years. Its members, mainly middle-class or educated black people or chiefs, thought the best way of achieving their aims was to keep on good terms with the whites, and win their respect by their reasonable behaviour. As members of the SANNC they had taken part in several deputations to London to put their case for a share in the government of South Africa (see page 26). As we have seen, these all came to nothing.

By 1930 the ANC was in the hands of moderate men like Pixley Seme. Its leaders were worried by members who became involved in anti-Pass Law protests, or the Communist Party. It needed a new generation of leaders to thrust it into the mainstream of resistance.

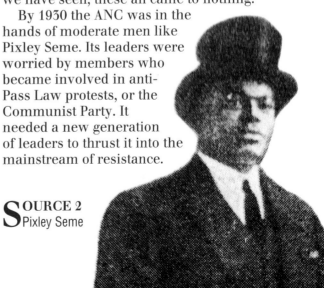

### SOURCE 2 Pixley Seme

1. Read Source 3. What is the attitude of Pixley Seme to his fellow black South Africans?
2. Use Source 3 and the rest of the information here to explain why the SANNC (and later the ANC) had so little mass appeal in these years.

**SOURCE 3** In 1930 Pixley Seme was elected President of the ANC. He outlined his hopes to a government enquiry

66 *The good policy to follow is to encourage the native to own property whenever possible. This would encourage thrift and enterprise among them. There is a great need for developing this class of native in urban areas to counteract the evils of rowdyism.* 99

## 2 How effective were anti-pass demonstrations?

One of the most hated segregation laws for many decades was the Pass Law. It reduced black people's ability to move freely and made them vulnerable to police harassment at any time. It turned every black person into a potential criminal.

When they were first introduced, passes only applied to men. There were few women in towns and an attempt to introduce passes for women in 1913 was met by a highly effective women's protest in Bloemfontein. This town was one of the few with near equal numbers of black men and women. Women held peaceful demonstrations and a mass burning of passes. An embarrassed government did not know how to handle the protest and withdrew the attempt to impose passes on women.

Many anti-pass demonstrations were held by men over the years, sometimes with wide support, but they were met with much tougher government opposition and did not succeed. Their effect, however, was to draw black Africans who had just arrived in the cities into political activity.

3. Why do you think women's anti-pass demonstrations were successful while demonstrations by men were not?

**SOURCE 4** Anti-pass demonstrators in Johannesburg in 1919. All the people in the crowd are under arrest

# 3 How effective was resistance by the Indian community?

Resistance by the Indian community was led by one of the most important figures in twentieth-century history, who lived in South Africa for over twenty years: Mohandas Gandhi. Gandhi was an Indian, who had trained in London as a lawyer. He arrived in South Africa from Britain to work with the Indian community in Natal in 1893. He was soon horrified at the blatant racism he found: he claimed to have been thrown out of a first-class railway carriage, even though he had a valid ticket, just because he was not white.

Gandhi began by supporting middle-class Indians against segregationist laws but was soon involved in mass protests. This led him to develop what he called *satyagraha* or 'soul-force', and we now call passive, or non-violent, resistance. This form of protest reflected his Hindu beliefs and was ideally suited to people who had no civil rights but large numbers. It involved large-scale, non-violent disobedience of the law. This led to mass arrests, which in turn flooded the courts and brought the work of the oppressive government to a standstill. Gandhi used *satyagraha* to great effect in India after his return there in 1914. The ANC adopted it; so did Martin Luther King in black civil rights protests in the USA, and many other protesters all over the world have used it in all kinds of situations.

In 1913 the government introduced a tax of £3 which was to be paid by all Indians. Gandhi organised a stay-at-home protest which involved most of the Indian community. Other grievances among the Indians led to a strike of 5,000 mine-workers and 15,000 sugar-plantation workers. Gandhi and other leaders were arrested. The government dealt with the strikers so violently that there was an international outcry. The South African government had to withdraw the new tax. Gandhi left South Africa in 1914 and returned to India to apply his ideas to winning freedom from British rule there.

**SOURCE 5** Gandhi at age 26, two years after he first arrived in South Africa

# 4 How effective was resistance from the trade unions?

Black workers saw how white trade unions were able to win wage increases and improved working conditions for their members. The first successful black trade union was the ICU, the Industrial and Commercial Union.

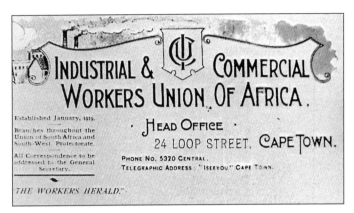

**SOURCE 6** The letterhead of the ICU, giving its address in Cape Town

**SOURCE 7** To black people ICU had another meaning

*66 To us Bantu it meant basically: when you ill-treat the African people, I See You; if you kick them off the pavements, I See You; I See You when you do not protect the Bantu; I See You when you kick my brother. 99*

The ICU began among the black dockworkers of Cape Town. In 1919 they went on strike for higher wages, led by Clements Kadalie. The strike was successful in winning wage increases and so was another one six months later. Kadalie linked up with other workers and soon the ICU included workers in all kinds of industries. They began to take up the grievances of rural Africans too, who were angry over losing their land.

By the mid-1920s there were perhaps 100,000 members, the majority of them from rural areas. But South Africa did not go the way of China, where Communist Party organisers from urban areas, with peasant support, were strong enough to take over the country in 1949. In South Africa the white government was more determined to crush the union. Kadalie was arrested and ICU branches closed down. There were quarrels between rival leaders and the ICU had collapsed by 1930.

# 5 How effective were the Communists?

Communism took hold among many groups of workers across the world in the late nineteenth and early twentieth centuries, particularly among miners. It was immigrant mineworkers who spread Communist ideas to South Africa. When the Russian Revolution of 1917 brought Lenin to power as leader of the first Communist government in the world, South African Communists celebrated on the steps of Johannesburg City Hall. The Communist Party of South Africa (CPSA) was set up in 1921. From the start it was the only political organisation in the country with both black and white members.

In the early years the CPSA supported white South African trade unions in the great miners' strike of 1922. These workers feared that the mine-owners would force their wages down by employing more black workers. This led to their extraordinary slogan: 'Workers of the World Unite for a White South Africa!' After the strike was fiercely crushed by the government, the CPSA tried to make links with the ANC and other black organisations, but most ANC leaders and chiefs were very suspicious of Communism. J.T. Gumede, who was more sympathetic towards Communism (see Source 9), was defeated as President of the ANC in 1930 by Pixley Seme. In the 1930s the CPSA had little influence, and by 1940 it had only 280 members.

**SOURCE 8** Government soldiers face striking workers, Johannesburg, 1922

**SOURCE 9** A comment made by J.T. Gumede, President of the ANC, in 1927

66 *The Communist Party alone has stood by us and protested when we have been shot down. The African has been a Communist from time immemorial. I have seen the new world come [in the USSR] where it has already begun.* 99

**SOURCE 10** A comment made by Chief Joseph Moshoeshoe of Matatiele, in 1928

66 *The Communist Party has brought Russia to the stage it is now. The Tsar was a great man in his country, of royal blood like us chiefs, and where is he now? It will be a sad day for me when I am ruled by the man who milks my cow or ploughs my fields.* 99

4. In what ways do Sources 9 and 10 differ?
5. Why do you think these two people reacted so differently to Communist ideas?
6. What do these differences tell us about the difficulties of achieving effective resistance to segregation?

# 6 How effective were segregationist black groups?

Some black South Africans supported segregation. They wanted as little as possible to do with whites. In the 1920s many followed Wellington Butelezi. He brought to South Africa the ideas of Marcus Garvey, a Jamaican living in the USA. Garvey called on black people all over the world to be independent of whites, and take pride in their ancestry.

### Black churches

Most of the Christian churches in South Africa were run by whites and many of them supported segregation. In the years after 1902 a huge number of new, independent black churches sprang up. Many black South Africans were deeply committed to these churches. It was a part of their lives that was not subject to white control.

## ■ TASK

Go back to our main enquiry: how effective was organised resistance to segregation before 1948? Look at the table you have completed (see Task on page 33). Make a judgement:

Resistance to segregation before 1948 **was/was** not successful. Therefore this **is/is not** a reason why the Nationalists won the 1948 election.

# How did the Second World War change South Africa?

YOU ARE NOW going to look at a second possible reason for the Nationalists' victory in the 1948 election: the effects of the Second World War on South Africa.

Although there was no fighting in South Africa, the war had a big impact on the country. South Africa was part of the British Empire and the Prime Minister, Jan Smuts, declared his support for Britain as soon as war broke out in 1939. Three hundred thousand South Africans fought in the war. Just over half of these – 186,000 – were whites; the black Africans who joined up were not allowed to carry weapons, but worked as labourers, orderlies, stretcher-bearers and so on.

**1.** Why do you think black Africans were allowed to join the South African armed forces but not allowed to fight?

## ■ ACTIVITY

Look at Sources 1, 2 and 3. You are a white South African soldier who has been away at war for five years, 1940–45. You have fought in North Africa and Italy. You have heard all about the Declaration of the new United Nations. Now you have come home. Write a letter to a friend from your army days, explaining how life in South Africa has changed and saying what you think about the changes.

The war helped South African industry. There were the armed forces to supply, and goods from abroad were scarce. With so many whites away at war, factories took on black workers or installed more machines. By the end of the war, South Africa had a modern, mechanised manufacturing industry, which had become more important than mining.

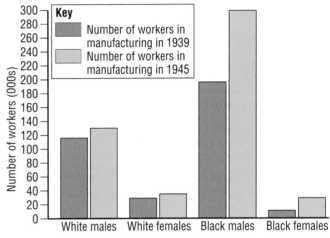

**SOURCE 2** Numbers of workers in manufacturing industry in South Africa in 1939 and 1945

**2.** Look at Source 2. Which groups of workers have shown the greatest increase?

**3.** Suggest reasons for the patterns that you see in these statistics.

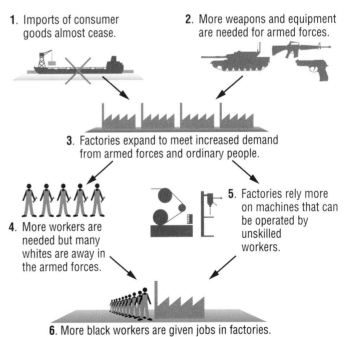

**SOURCE 3** The effects of the war on manufacturing industry in South Africa

**SOURCE 1** Black print workers in Pretoria, 1944

## Changes in government policy

By 1946 there were more blacks than whites in urban areas for the first time. The average wage in industry for blacks was £128 a year: hardly enough to live on, but better than the £32 a year average in farming. This movement of black people to the cities was made easier by changes in government policy.

Many Afrikaners had wanted to keep South Africa neutral in the war. They objected to fighting on Britain's side and some Afrikaner politicians left Smuts' government. People of British descent had more influence and the government became more liberal in attitude. Smuts was friendly with leaders of manufacturing industry and tried to meet their needs.

- Pass Laws were relaxed.
- Money was put into black education (because employers wanted educated workers).
- A health programme for all races was discussed (because employers wanted healthy workers).
- Food prices were kept low (because employers did not want to pay high wages).
- A report looked into: 'Ways, other than increasing wages, of improving the economic, social and health conditions of natives in urban areas'.

## Black reactions

Black people took the opportunity of being really needed by the white economy to press for improvements in their condition.

- There were bus boycotts when bus companies tried to increase fares from black townships some distance from city centres.
- The South African Indian Congress organised effective, mass, non-violent resistance to the 'Ghetto Act' of 1945. This was an attempt by the government to restrict the rights of Indians to live and own property wherever they liked.
- There were strikes in several industries (see Source 4). Most alarming for the government was the mineworkers' strike of August 1946. The miners, living in their compounds, out of touch with other mines, under the supervision of their employers and cut off from the outside world, were difficult to organise. Yet 73,000 miners, from 21 mines, took part in the strike. Smuts' government acted ferociously, supporting the mine-owners. Nine miners were killed and the strike was crushed in four days.

**SOURCE 4** Police address strikers, 1946

**SOURCE 5** Moses Kotane, President of the African Mineworkers Union, writing in 1945

*66 The gold-mining industry employs over 348,000 African workers. These workers are recruited from landless, poverty-stricken, heavily-taxed and backward peasants in the reserves. These workers produced gold worth 108 million rand, with a profit of 40 million. But they received only a meagre wage of 5.72 rand a month. 685 died as a result of accidents. 1498 died as a result of disease. Every year thousands more die of miners' phthisis [a lung disease] contracted in the mines and in most instances the dependants receive no compensation. 99*

| Year | Strikes | White workers involved | Black workers involved | Working days lost |
|------|---------|------------------------|------------------------|-------------------|
| 1940 | 24 | 1,200 | 700 | 6,500 |
| 1941 | 35 | 700 | 4,800 | 23,200 |
| 1942 | 58 | 1,300 | 12,800 | 49,500 |
| 1943 | 52 | 1,800 | 7,400 | 47,700 |
| 1944 | 52 | 200 | 12,000 | 62,700 |
| 1945 | 63 | 1,500 | 14,700 | 91,100 |

**S**OURCE 6  Strikes in South Africa 1940–45

The slight improvement in their conditions and the effectiveness of their protests led some blacks to be optimistic about change in South Africa and winning some civil rights. Some were encouraged by the Declaration of the United Nations, which was drawn up in 1942 and in which Smuts played a big part. It spoke of liberty, equality and democracy.

4. Why do you think the number of black protests increased at a time when black people were doing better than in previous years?

### ■ ACTIVITY

Write a Strategy Briefing Paper for the leaders of the National Party as the 1948 election approaches on how the country has changed since the Second World War started. Your briefing should contain key points only. You must produce it in as few words as possible. It should have three parts.

**Part 1:** Write two or three points which sum up the effects of the war on the South African economy.

**Part 2:** Write three or four points which sum up the changes the war has brought for black people and how they have reacted.

**Part 3:** Put forward three points which the National Party should make to white voters in order to gain their support.

### ■ TALKING POINT

So far, which seems the more important factor in winning support for the National Party in 1948:

- the need to crush black resistance
- reversing the changes caused by the Second World War?

**S**OURCE 7  Armed police clash with strikers at a mineworkers' strike march, 1946

# How did the National Party appeal to white voters?

WE NOW COME to the third possible explanation for the Nationalists' victory in 1948 – their appeal to white voters.

## The rise of the Afrikaners

Although the Afrikaners formed the majority of whites in South Africa, they had always been individualists, keeping themselves to themselves. They had no real sense of unity as a people. After 1902, their defeat in the South African War, the deaths of so many of their relatives and the attempt to suppress their language led to the forging of an Afrikaner identity.

### ■ TASK

1. Why was there no real Afrikaner identity before the twentieth century?
2. What difficulties would there be in uniting all Afrikaners?
3. Explain how each of the five factors in Source 2 helped to build and support Afrikaner unity.

1. In Source 3, who are the 'strangers [who] now want to trample us underfoot'?

The emphasis on a chosen people and racial superiority had much in common with the Nazi movement in Germany, which was rising to power at the same time. Several Afrikaners were keen supporters of the Nazis. They included Dr Verwoerd and John Vorster, who both later became Prime Ministers of South Africa.

The year 1938 seemed a great opportunity for Afrikaners, keen to make the most of their history, to celebrate the centenary of the Battle of Blood River, and their vow (see page 13). The Voortrekker Monument was built, showing the taking of the vow. Two wagons carrying men, women and children dressed in Boer costume set off from Cape Town for the Monument. In every town they passed through, people flocked to see these 'trekkers'.

SOURCE 1 Crowds in nineteenth century Boer costume greet one of the two wagons of 'trekkers' on its way to the Voortrekker Monument as part of the celebrations for the centenary of the Battle of Blood River, 1938

## Finance

In 1918 wealthier Afrikaners helped to set up Afrikaner insurance and saving companies, called Santam and Sanlam. The aim was to help Afrikaners start up their own businesses without having to rely on British-controlled banks.

**S**OURCE 3 An extract from *The History of our country in the language of our people*, 1876, explaining the book's aims

*66 To make our children familiar from an early age with what their forefathers had to go through and what they suffered in this land where strangers now want to trample us underfoot. 99*

## Publishing

- A history of the Afrikaners, in Afrikaans.
- A popular magazine, *Die Huisgenoot* (*The Home Companion*). It was intended to reach ordinary Afrikaners, perhaps living on isolated farms, and give them a sense of unity with the rest of the Afrikaner people.
- An Afrikaner newspaper, *De Burger*.

# How did Afrikaners develop a sense of unity?

The powder horn, the symbol of the National Party. Horns like these were used by Trekboers to hold gunpowder

## Politics

The National Party, formed in 1914, set out to win the support of all Afrikaners, rich and poor, farmers and business people.

## Secret society

The BROEDERBOND, formed in 1918 in Johannesburg and dedicated to uniting and supporting Afrikaners:

- particularly sought out men in positions of influence to become members
- tried to ensure Afrikaners were promoted
- had a secret handshake, so that members could identify each other
- had 500 members by 1930, mainly in Transvaal.

At its ceremonies the British flag was spread over a table and covered by the South African flag.

## The Church

The Dutch Reformed Church (the Church of the Afrikaners):

- gave Biblical support to Afrikaner views on the racial superiority of whites
- set up schools so that Afrikaner children could be taught in Afrikaans.

**S**OURCE 2 Factors that helped to develop Afrikaner unity

## How did the National Party appeal to whites?

### White grievances

White South Africans were feeling disgruntled in the years just after the Second World War. There were several reasons for this.

- The economy was in difficulties as it readjusted to peacetime conditions. For a while, jobs were scarce. White workers returning from the war found black workers in jobs they had regarded as theirs. They found that black wages had risen from one-fifth of white wages to 'only' a quarter.
- White farmers resented the policy of keeping food prices low, which Smuts had introduced in the war years. They also resented the flood of black workers to the cities, where they could earn good wages; farmers wanted cheap black labour.

S OURCE 4  Farm labourers picking oranges

- They were shocked at black protests and strikes. They hated and feared black resistance and Smuts did not seem to be able to 'keep the black man in his place', as they put it.
- They read about Smuts talking of liberty and democracy while he was abroad. In fact he left his ideals at the airport when he returned to South Africa but, increasingly, whites distrusted him. They were angry at the new United Nations for criticising their racist policies.

### Nationalist promises

For Nationalist Afrikaner intellectuals, teachers, clerics and Broederbond members Malan promised a white South Africa under Afrikaner rule, with blacks removed to the reserves.

For white workers he held out the danger of the 'black threat', to jobs, law and order, and housing.

S OURCE 5  Dr Daniel Malan, leader of the National Party, and Prime Minister 1948–56

But for white industrialists he promised a more 'flexible' apartheid, with blacks allowed, under strict controls, to leave the reservations temporarily to work in the cities.

For white farmers, a supply of cheap black labour was promised.

**S**OURCE 6  Smuts made clear his policy on racial segregation in South Africa in 1945

*❝ It is a fixed policy to maintain white supremacy in South Africa, maintaining our white civilisation and keeping our white race pure. ❞*

Smuts seemed to be unable to hold the whites together under his leadership. Dr Malan managed to unite enough of them to win. The Sauer Report outlined apartheid, but in vague terms, so that many whites from different backgrounds and with different beliefs could find in it something for them.

**S**OURCE 7  Malan in a cartoon from an Afrikaner newspaper in 1945. *Swart gevaar* means 'black threat' in Afrikaans

**The result**

Afrikaner Party 9 seats

Other parties 9 seats (total)

National Party 70 seats

United Party 65 seats

**S**OURCE 8  The National Party won only 39 per cent of the votes in 1948, but it was enough to become the largest party in Parliament. Two-thirds of the Afrikaners voted for them, but the National Party would not have won without the support of 20 per cent of English-speaking South Africans too

## ■ SUMMARY TASK

'The most important factor in the National Party's election victory in 1948 was that they united all Afrikaner voters.' Do you agree with this statement? Explain your answer.

Use your answers to the Tasks on pages 36 and 40 to start you off. Did the Nationalists win because:

■ organised black resistance was becoming too effective?

■ the Second World War had changed the country in ways many whites did not like?
■ they united all Afrikaners?
■ they united all whites?

Use your answers to these little questions to help you answer the BIG question. Start with a simple yes or no to each, then give your reasons. End by describing the ways the statement at the top is right and the ways it is not right, or not the whole answer.

# chapter 4

# WHAT WAS APARTHEID?

**Apartheid means separateness**

# Introduction

> A housemaid, Mathilda Chikuye, was fined 30 rand for having her husband in her room at 20 Talbrager Avenue, Johannesburg.

> A garage mechanic, Thabane Ntshiwa, was sentenced to four months in prison for having 'Free Nelson Mandela' scratched on his tea mug.

THE NEWS ITEMS above appeared in South African newspapers in the 1980s.

What kind of system fines a woman for having her husband in her room?

What kind of system imprisons a man for having a slogan scratched on his tea mug?

Both of these events happened because the two people had broken the laws of the system of apartheid, which began in South Africa in 1948.

In this chapter the first question we must ask is: 'What was apartheid?'

But there are other questions to be asked and answered. People have made a lot of claims about apartheid. It is the job of historians to examine the things people say to see if they are historically accurate. So we will examine four questions which historians have tried to answer about apartheid.

1 Was there anything new about apartheid?

Apartheid is a completely new policy, created by us, the National Party.

2 Was apartheid all planned from the start?

3 Did apartheid change under Verwoerd?

**WHAT WAS APARTHEID?**

Apartheid was all planned from the start – the Nationalists were working to a master plan!

4 Apartheid did seem to be collapsing by the late 1980s. Was it always bound to fail?

It was obvious that apartheid could not last for ever – its collapse was inevitable.

Dr Verwoerd, who was Prime Minister from 1958 to 1966, made big changes to the apartheid system.

**1950** Population Registration Act
**1950** Group Areas Act

**Johannes Strijdom**
1956–58

| Daniel Malan 1948–56 | Hendrik Verwoerd 1958–66 | Balthazar Johannes Vorster 1966–78 |
|---|---|---|

**1952** Abolition of Passes Act
**1953** Separate Amenities Act
**1953** Bantu Education Act

**SOURCE 1** A timeline showing South African Prime Ministers 1948–78 and key acts of the 1950s

# How did apartheid affect people's lives?

## ■ TASK

1. Here are some sources showing how people were affected by apartheid. Discuss what is happening in each case. Try to reach some first thoughts about what apartheid was like.
2. As you read about the laws of apartheid over the next six pages try to match each of Sources 2–8 to the law which caused it.

SOURCE 5  Military trucks moving people out of Sophiatown, Johannesburg, 1955

SOURCE 2  The story of Regina Brooks

❝ Regina Brooks was a woman classified as a white, who lived with a Zulu, the father of her child, in Orlando township. The police found out and raided their house in the middle of the night. The white sergeant jumped into their bedroom through the window. Tried at Johannesburg Magistrates Court in November 1955, they were both sent to prison for four months. ❞

SOURCE 6  Dr Verwoerd, Prime Minister of South Africa 1958–66, speaking in 1952

❝ The white South African's duty to the native is to Christianise him and help him culturally. Native education should be based on the principles of non-equality and segregation. The native will be taught from childhood that equality is not for them. People who believe that are not suitable teachers of natives. ❞

SOURCE 3  Regina Brooks with her partner, Richard Kumalo, and their baby

SOURCE 7  A policeman stopping someone to look at his pass

SOURCE 4  Signs in a park indicating areas people were allowed to enter

SOURCE 8  An anti-apartheid protester being held under house arrest

# $H$ ow did the Nationalists introduce apartheid?

MALAN'S NATIONAL PARTY had won the 1948 election on the basis of their policy of apartheid. Over the next few years a series of laws was passed to make South Africa a racially separated country.

## 1. Laws to define a person's race and prevent any more people of mixed race being born

- **Prohibition of Mixed Marriages Act, 1949:** made marriages between people of different races illegal.
- **Immorality Act, 1950:** made sexual relations between different races illegal.
- **Population Registration Act, 1950:** defined which race every South African belonged to.

Thirty years later population registration was still in force. People could apply to be reclassified, involving a bizarre inspection of skin, nails and hair. In 1984–85, 518 Coloureds were reclassified white; fourteen whites became Coloured; seven Chinese became white; two whites became Chinese; three Malays became white; a white became an Indian; seventeen Indians became Malay; one Malay became Chinese; 89 blacks became Coloured and five Coloureds became black.

## 2. Laws to separate the races in public areas and on public transport

- **Separate Amenities Act, 1953:** this is often called 'PETTY APARTHEID' – the division of public services and spaces according to race. This meant separate parks, beaches, post offices, railway trains, buses, toilets, cinemas and seating areas at sporting events.

1. There was often a clash between the wish to separate the races and the needs of industry. How does Source 1 illustrate this?
2. What does Source 3 tell us about:
a) separation of the races?
b) inequality between races?
3. Apartheid cost the country money. What costs were involved in the situations depicted in Sources 1 and 3?

**SOURCE 1** From the newspaper *Cape Times*, 13 December 1960

*❝ At a cost of several thousands of pounds, a new subway for railway workers has been built to connect Salt River station with the Salt River Railway workshops. It will enable white and non-white workers to arrive at the workshops through different subways. But having arrived through their different subways, white and non-white workers will continue to work side by side inside the workshop. ❞*

**SOURCE 2** A beach sign at Port Elizabeth. This 4 km stretch of beach was split into areas for Europeans, Malays, Indians, Chinese and Coloureds

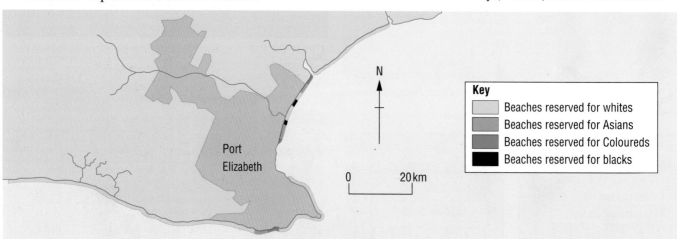

**SOURCE 3** A map showing how beaches around Port Elizabeth were divided into areas for use by different races

# 3. Laws to separate where the races lived

■ **Group Areas Act, 1950:** each town or city was separated into 'white', 'Coloured' and 'black' areas.

Under this law, lines were drawn on town and city maps all over the country. If you were living in the 'wrong' area, you had to move. Usually it was black and Coloured people who had to move: out of 3.5 million people who had to leave their homes under this Act between 1951 and 1986, only 2 per cent were white.

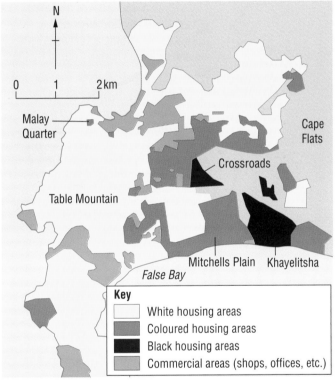

**S**OURCE 4  A map of Cape Town, showing how the city was separated into 'white', 'Coloured' and 'black' areas of housing

## Sophiatown
Sophiatown, in Johannesburg, was an area near the centre of the city where black people had owned their own housing, or rented it from black owners, for a long time. It was poor, but it was a community and people liked living there. In its clubs some of the greatest South African musicians and poets had grown up and won their audiences. It was declared a 'white' area under the Group Areas Act and people were forcibly moved to the township of Soweto. The place that was once Sophiatown became a white suburb called Triomf (which means 'Triumph' in Afrikaans).

**S**OURCE 5  Father Trevor Huddleston, a white Anglican monk, lived in Sophiatown. In this extract from his book, *Naught For Your Comfort*, he describes the day the government moved the people out of Sophiatown

*66 10th February, 1955. Lining the street were thousands of police ... a few Sten guns were in position at various points ... Already the lorries were piled high with the pathetic possessions which had come from the row of rooms in the background ... In a few years Sophiatown will cease to exist. It will be, first of all, a rubbish heap, laying low the houses, good and bad alike, that I have known, emptying them of the life, the laughter and the tears of children, until the place is a grey ruin lying in the sun ... And in a few years men will have forgotten that this was a living community, and a very unusual one. 99*

4. Look again at Source 5 on page 45 and read Source 5 above.
a) What differences are there between these two sources?
b) Which is more useful to you in finding out about the removal of people from Sophiatown in 1955?

## District Six
District Six was an area of Cape Town with a mixed-race population. Most people were Coloureds, and it had been a Coloured area since 1860, but whites, blacks, Jews, Muslims and Indians lived there too. It was a poor area, with old, run-down housing, but like Sophiatown it was a real community. It was designated 'white' and gradually the people were separated and moved out. Large numbers of people were involved in the District Six removals: 60,000 Coloureds had to go and live several kilometres away in new housing at Mitchells Plain.

**S**OURCE 6  An extract from the oral accounts of the removal of blacks from District Six in Cape Town, collected by the University of Cape Town

*66 Question: What do you feel about the Group Areas Act which moved you from District Six?*
*Answer: Oooo, don't talk about that. I will start to cry. I will cry all over again. That's when the trouble started ... when they chucked us out of Cape Town. My whole life ... changed ... What they took away they can never give back. I was far away from my family. All the neighbours were strangers. That was the hardest part, believe me ... They destroyed us. 99*

5. Read Source 8. The government official feels he has done a good job for the people of District Six. How would he use Source 7 to support his case?
6. What might the person interviewed in Source 6 say about Source 7?
7. a) What caption might the government official in Source 8 write for Source 9?
   b) What caption would you write for Source 9?

**SOURCE 8** The views of the government official responsible for moving Coloured families out of District Six

❝ *I'm not ashamed to say I was responsible for District Six being wiped out – in fact, I'm proud of it. Those poor people who lived in squalor in District Six – a slum of slums – are now far better off. Mitchells Plain is a striking example of how one's lot in life can be bettered.* ❞

**SOURCE 7** District Six housing before forced removals under the Group Areas Act

**SOURCE 9** The area of District Six, cleared and still unoccupied in 1982

# 4. Laws to separate the races in schools

There were several aspects to the **Bantu Education Act, 1953**.

- All schools were brought under state control. Previously, missionaries had provided many schools. The education in them varied but some were very good; many black resistance leaders owed their education to a good mission school. Now the government wanted to control what was taught.
- Less money was spent on black pupils: in 1953 it was 63.92 rands per white pupil and 8.99 rands per black pupil. This meant larger classes, more dilapidated buildings and less-qualified teachers. Black children were not expected to continue their education beyond primary level.
- Black children had a different curriculum from whites. They were taught about white superiority and that black South Africans belonged in their ethnic groups. They were often taught in their ethnic language, not English. They were mostly just taught the skills needed to get a menial job in the black homelands.

The man responsible for working all this out was Dr Hendrick Verwoerd, Minister for Native Affairs, who became Prime Minister from 1958 to 1966.

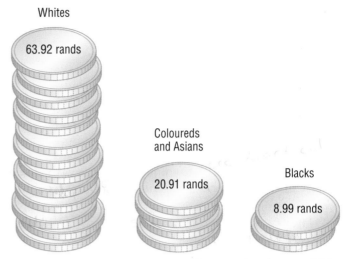

Whites
63.92 rands

Coloureds and Asians
20.91 rands

Blacks
8.99 rands

**SOURCE 12** Government spending on education per child, 1953

**SOURCE 13** A classroom under the Bantu education system

**SOURCE 10** Verwoerd describes his view of education for black children in 1953. (Note that he describes black people as BANTU. This term was resented by black South Africans)

*66 What is the use of teaching the Bantu mathematics when he cannot use it in practice? There is no place for the Bantu above a certain level of labour. 99*

**SOURCE 11** Another comment by Verwoerd, in 1954

*66 It is no use giving [a black person] a training which has as its aim absorption into the European community, where he cannot be absorbed. Until now he has been subjected to a school system which drew him away from his own community and misled him by showing him the green pastures of European society in which he is not allowed to graze. 99*

**SOURCE 14** Albert Lutuli, President of the ANC 1952–67, describes black parents' dilemma under Bantu education

*66 The choice before parents is an almost impossible one – they do not want the Bantu education and they do not want their children on the streets. They have to choose between two evils. 99*

8. What did Verwoerd want black children to learn?
9. What did he *not* want them to learn?
10. In what ways would the education system he describes in Sources 10 and 11 support and reinforce apartheid?
11. In Source 14, Lutuli describes the parents' choice as 'almost impossible'. Why was it such a dilemma for them?

## 5. Laws to divide the entire country into 'black' and 'white' areas

The most drastic apartheid policy was to work towards excluding blacks from white areas completely. Gradually blacks would be forced to take up residence in the black 'reserves'. If they did come into a 'white' area to work, they would be temporary migrants, with no political or any other rights. 'INFLUX CONTROL', as it was called, would put tough restrictions on any new black people coming into urban areas.

> **S**OURCE 15 A National Party MP in 1960 describes the position of blacks in urban areas
>
> *66 They are only supplying a commodity, the commodity of labour. It is labour we are importing, not labourers as individuals. 99*

**12.** How does the speaker in Source 15 think of black workers?

- **Bantu Authorities Act, 1951:** this gave the government the power to appoint tribal chiefs who ruled the reserves. These reserves still covered only 13 per cent of the area of South Africa, although black people made up almost 70 per cent of the total population.
- **Native Laws Amendment Act, 1952:** this was intended to bring in strict influx control. Special labour bureaux were set up to control the movement of workers, restrict those allowed into urban areas and force employers to give priority in jobs to blacks already in urban areas.

However, the law did acknowledge that some blacks had been living in urban areas for a long time. Under Section 10 of the **Native Urban Areas Act, 1954** a black person was allowed to live in an urban area if:

- he (it nearly always applied to men) had been born there and had lived there ever since
- he had lived there for fifteen years and committed no offence
- he had worked there for the same employer for ten years
- he or she was the child or wife of someone allowed to stay in an urban area.

This was quite a loophole in strict apartheid as it gave many black people an absolute right to live in a town.

- **Abolition of Passes Act, 1952:** despite its name, this Act extended the pass system to cover all blacks in urban areas. Eventually, despite protests, it was extended to include women, too. If black people were in an urban area without proper authorisation in their passbook they would be fined and sent to their reserve or 'homeland'.

The pass system was one of the most resented aspects of apartheid. It allowed police to stop black people at any time and demand to see their pass. They were assumed guilty unless they could prove they were innocent, a reversal of an important human right. It was hard to keep the passes up to date and thousands were arrested: 384,497 people in 1962 alone.

'YOU'RE ALL UNDER ARREST!'

**S**OURCE 16 A cartoon about arrests under the Pass Laws, 1962

## 6. Laws to crush opposition

■ **Suppression of Communism Act, 1950:** this banned the South African Communist Party, but actually had very little to do with Communism. By 1950 the Western world was engaged in a struggle with the USSR known as the Cold War. It was seen as a struggle between capitalism and Communism, and many people believed that the USSR was intent on spreading Communism all over the world. South Africa fully supported the West in the Cold War and the National Party labelled as 'Communism' any serious opposition. Believing in racial equality, for example, was 'Communist'. The Suppression of Communism Act gave the government extra powers: to arrest and hold people without charge, to 'ban' them, so that they could not meet others or take part in politics, or to put them under house arrest. (To find out more on how this aspect of apartheid worked, see page 74.)

### ■ TASK 1

Apartheid means separateness, but the laws outlined on pages 46–51 clearly set up a system which was not only separate but unequal. One of the terms used to describe these laws is *baaskap*, meaning 'white supremacy'.

Look at each of the six aspects of apartheid on pages 46–51. Did they lead to unequal treatment of blacks and whites? In what ways? Your teacher will give you a sheet to record your answers.

### ■ TASK 2

**Was there anything new about apartheid?**
Dr Xuma, who was President of the ANC in 1948, said: 'The apartheid policy of the National Party is nothing new and should be nothing surprising to any honest and serious student of coloured relations. It is a mere elaboration, a natural and logical growth of the South African native policy.' Was Dr Xuma right?

We are going to decide whether apartheid was new or just a continuation of what went on before.

1. First, look at each of the apartheid laws to see which, if any, of the human rights outlined in the Declaration on pages 4–5 it broke.
2. We can then compare whether each of these human rights was safe before apartheid. To do this, you will need to look back over Chapter 2 (pages 22–31).
3. Record your results on your own copy of the table below.

| Law | Human right broken (give number) | Was this right safe before apartheid? (yes/no) |
| --- | --- | --- |
| Prohibition of Mixed Marriages Act, 1949 | | |
| Group Areas Act, 1950 | | |
| Immorality Act, 1950 | | |
| Population Registration Act, 1950 | | |
| Suppression of Communism Act, 1950 | | |
| Bantu Authorities Act, 1951 | | |
| Abolition of Passes Act, 1952 | | |
| Native Laws Amendment Act, 1952 | | |
| Bantu Education Act, 1953 | | |
| Separate Amenities Act, 1953 | | |
| Native Urban Areas Act, 1954 | | |

4. Now use the information from the table to decide where each of the laws should be placed on the spectrum line below. Mark their positions on your own copy of the spectrum line.

5. 'Apartheid was new because it made it clear that black South Africans were going to be deprived of several of their human rights.' As a class, hold a debate on this statement.

| Completely new | Going a lot further than before | Going a bit further than before | Nothing new |
| --- | --- | --- | --- |

# Was apartheid all planned from the start?

*❝ There has been <u>nothing haphazard</u> about apartheid... Operating on the basis of <u>an agreed belief</u>, the Nationalists have planned their strategy with care and <u>worked step by step towards their goal</u>. ❞*

WAS BUNTING RIGHT? From his point of view, apartheid must indeed have looked as if it was worked out to some horrifying master-plan, gradually but unstoppably being put into practice through the series of laws described on pages 46–51. But we are now going to look at some evidence showing that it wasn't quite like that. We will look in turn at each of the phrases underlined in Source 1.

## ■ TASK 1

1. As you read through Points 1–4 below, think about whether the idea of apartheid all being planned from the start still seems accurate.
2. Write a sentence for each point, summarising how it fits in with the idea of a master-plan. Your teacher will give you a sheet to help you.

## 1. An agreed belief?

A master-plan suggests that people agreed in advance what should be done. But we have already seen in Chapter 3 (page 43) that the National Party was deliberately vague about exactly what apartheid meant, in order to gain support in the 1948 election. There were really two approaches to apartheid, as Source 2 shows.

**A Idealist apartheid**

Blacks and whites must be totally separated.

We must work towards a situation in which blacks and whites will live in separate areas of the country.

Blacks will live in their tribal homelands, ruling themselves to a limited extent. They will earn their living by farming.

Whites will control mining and industry but employ no black workers. All jobs in industry will be done by white workers, or by machines.

**B Practical apartheid**

Blacks and whites must be separated as far as possible.

Our high standard of living depends on industry, which has always employed large numbers of black workers. We shall always need black labour because it is cheap and so our goods can be sold around the world at competitive prices.

We prefer to use black migrant workers from the reserves because then we don't have to pay wages high enough to support the workers' families.

SOURCE 2 Two different approaches to apartheid

■ **TASK 2**

Read through Sources 3–7. All of them were written or spoken by National Party members or supporters. As you read them, decide whether they support **A** (idealist apartheid) or **B** (practical apartheid).

**SOURCE 3**  A farmer, speaking in 1948

❝ *Non-white workers are now so enmeshed in every sphere of our economic life that for 500 or 1,000 years, if not longer, total segregation is pure wishful thinking.* ❞

**SOURCE 4**  The views of the Dutch Reformed Church on the goal the government should be aiming for, 1959

❝ *Complete reorganisation of the existing economic structure so that all industries would in time be manned wholly by whites.* ❞

**SOURCE 5**  Cornelius Mulder, Minister of Native Affairs, speaking in 1976

❝ *The goal is that eventually there will be no black South Africans.* ❞

**SOURCE 6**  Dr Malan, Prime Minister, explains the National Party's position in 1950

❝ *Total segregation is not the policy of our party. Total territorial separation is impracticable under present circumstances in South Africa where our whole economic structure is based on native labour.* ❞

**SOURCE 7**  A Bantu Affairs Department spokesman explaining the situation in 1967

❝ *It is government policy that Bantu are only temporarily resident in European areas for as long as they offer their labour there. As soon as they become no longer fit to work, or are not needed, they are expected to return to their homeland.* ❞

## 2. Nothing haphazard?

The National government of 1948 had no experience of government. They had a majority of only five seats over other parties and could not be sure of winning another election. They had to try to keep the support of all the different groups who had voted for them. A government in that position cannot afford to work to a master-plan.

The laws described on pages 46–51 were introduced as opportunities arose. The fact that some were passed fairly soon after the Nationalists took power, while others came later, was just the way things happened, rather than part of an overall plan.

The laws described on pages 46–51 do not fit together properly. Verwoerd's policy for education (see page 49) is clearly 'idealist apartheid'. The influx control policy (page 50) was 'practical apartheid'. Indeed, Section 10 of the Native Laws Amendment Act gave blacks the right to stay in urban areas, which was the last thing many apartheid supporters wanted.

## 3. Moving steadily towards their goal?

The influx control system never worked as planned. Employers were supposed to hire blacks through the government labour bureaux. They were supposed to give priority to black workers who already lived in urban areas in order to reduce the flow of new black workers moving into urban areas. But most employers ignored the labour bureaux and did their own hiring. They preferred blacks from the reserves because they could pay them less and because these blacks were utterly dependent on their white employers.

The influx control policy was a failure: the number of black workers in urban areas went up from 2.3 million to 3.4 million during the 1950s.

## 4. Step by step?

The Prime Minister from 1958 to 1966 was Dr Verwoerd. Under his leadership a new wave of apartheid laws was brought in. The fact that Verwoerd's apartheid is so different from what went before shows that the National Party did not have a master-plan which was systematically put into effect.

# How did apartheid change under Verwoerd?

WHICH OF THE two apartheid ideas, **A** or **B** (see page 52), did Verwoerd support? Read again what he said when he was Minister for Native Affairs in the 1950s (Sources 10 and 11 on page 49) and Source 2 below.

Verwoerd promised his supporters that South Africa would be an all-white country by 1978. He was able to take a different course for his 'second phase' apartheid from the one taken by Malan in 1948 for a number of reasons, as Source 2 explains.

**SOURCE 1** Dr Hendrick Verwoerd, Prime Minister of South Africa 1958–66

**SOURCE 2** Verwoerd's view of South Africa's future under apartheid

*❝ If South Africa has to choose between being poor and white or rich and multiracial, then it must choose to be white. ❞*

## The creation of the Bantustans

The key to Verwoerd's vision of an all-white South Africa was his policy for the black homelands, which are also known as BANTUSTANS. In 1955 Professor Tomlinson presented the results of a long inquiry he had been carrying out into how to make 'idealist apartheid' work. He proposed that:

- the black reserves (the 13 per cent of the country identified in the 1936 Land Act – see page 27) should be increased in size and become black 'homelands'
- the South African government should spend money (he calculated that it would cost over £100 million) to improve farming and establish industries in these homelands.

After a time, these black homelands would be able to support all black South Africans, who would then be excluded from white South Africa.

To what extent did Verwoerd put the recommendations of the Tomlinson Report into practice? By the **Bantu Self-Government Act, 1959**, eight self-governing homelands were created. (This number was later increased to ten.) Each was intended to be the homeland of a particular ethnic group (although there were two for the Xhosa people). With black South Africans divided between ten 'independent' homelands, whites would be the largest single racial group in South Africa – a majority at last! The assassination of Verwoerd in 1966 prevented him from seeing the Bantustans fully established. However, John Vorster, his successor as

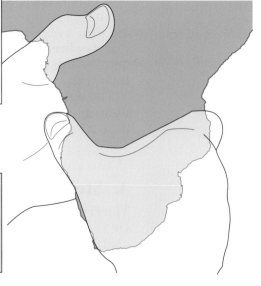

1. The National Party won over half of all votes cast in the 1958 election. Apartheid seemed to be very popular with whites: not just the Afrikaners, but the English-speaking whites too. The National Party's political position was much stronger than it had been in 1948.

2. The National Party carried out a policy of promoting Afrikaners to key jobs. By 1958 they controlled much of the civil service, local government, the armed forces, the police, newspapers, radio stations, the legal system and some universities.

3. Members of the Broederbond were promoted, particularly in departments that dealt with relations with blacks, such as the Ministry of Native Affairs. 'Idealist' apartheid ideas dominated the policies of this department.

4. Opposition to apartheid in the British Commonwealth led to strained relations and Britain had less influence on South African affairs. (South Africa left the Commonwealth in 1961.)

5. The government became more willing to use force to crush opposition. The police force increased in size by 25 per cent between 1946 and 1955. Most of its officers were Afrikaners and strong supporters of white supremacy.

**SOURCE 3** How the National Party strengthened its grip on South Africa, 1948–58

S

Prime Minister, pursued the same policy and led the first Bantustans to 'independence' in 1976. Although the Bantustans were supposed to be the homelands of all black South Africans, many of their people continued to live and work outside them: 18 per cent of the people who were registered as having Transkei as their 'home' lived outside it; 78 per cent of the people of the tiny scrap of land called the QwaQwa homeland lived in 'white' South Africa. No country in the world recognised the Bantustans as independent states. Why not?

As the map shows, some homelands were tiny, others were divided fragments of land (Bophuthatswana was split into six different bits, KwaZulu into 26). Tomlinson's proposal to round them up in size was not, on the whole, carried out.

They were propped up by huge amounts of money from the South African government. Ciskei, for example, one of the poorest regions in South Africa, had a new capital city built – Bisho – with a casino, shopping centre, offices, Parliament building, presidential palace and large houses for government ministers, at a cost of 59 million rand. It also has an international airport, costing 25 million rand, at which no plane has yet landed.

Under pressure from white industrialists, Verwoerd did not allow industry to develop in the Bantustans.

Pressure from white farmers prevented the government from investing in farming improvements.

**S**OURCE 4 An extract from the speech made by M.C. Botha, Minister of Bantu Affairs, in 1976, when Transkei became the first 'independent' homeland

*66 It is the dawn of an exceptionally unique day; the day on which South Africa, for the first time, takes the necessary step to give up its guardianship over one of its wards by declaring it to be independent . . . A day of fulfilment for the National Party. 99*

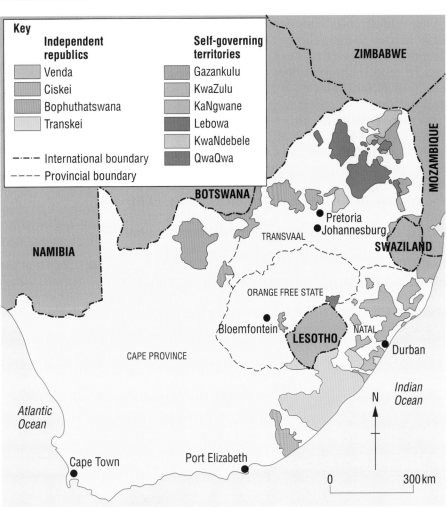

**S**OURCE 5 A map showing the black homelands in 1989. Note that only four had been granted 'independence' by this time

They did not have democratically elected governments. The black rulers of the Bantustans were chosen by the chiefs, whose choice had to be approved by the South African government.

The Bantustans had all the symbols of an independent country, such as a flag and an anthem, but the South African government still controlled their foreign and defence policies. Verwoerd said it would be 2,000 years before they could be completely self-governing.

## How did the growth of the Bantustans affect people in South Africa?

### The rulers

The rulers of the Bantustans drew big salaries as Presidents or Prime Ministers and had plentiful opportunities to make money on the side. For example, Kaiser Matanzima, President of Transkei, was 'granted' several farms, supposedly for the part he had played in the 'struggle for independence'.

The rulers of the Bantustans tried to create a black middle class who depended on them for their high wages and standard of living. The average income of someone in Transkei in 1970 was 169 rand a month but members of the governing council claimed annual salaries of 12,000 rand, as well as extra allowances and travelling expenses. Lots of jobs were created for government officials: in 1963 there were 2,446 officials in Transkei; by 1980 there were over 20,000. Teachers were paid good salaries and received pay rises totalling 189 per cent between 1962 and 1978. But they had to teach the same white-dominated curriculum as was used in the rest of South Africa.

South African government money was used to offer tremendous incentives to white businesses to invest in the Bantustans. The black ruling class did well out of this but few jobs were created for ordinary workers. The most remarkable Bantustan investment was Sun City. This casino and nightclub complex in Bophuthatswana was built by a white businessman and attracted thousands of white visitors from South Africa, where gambling was forbidden. It even attracted international entertainers.

**S**OURCE 6   The famous American singer Frank Sinatra visited Sun City in 1981 and seems to have swallowed the information he was given

  *The whole government is black and is an equal partner of Sol Kerzner [the white owner of Sun City]. Bophuthatswana gets 50 cents on every rand that goes into a Sun City slot machine. Furthermore, Sol has given much-needed employment to 3,000 black Tswana tribesmen.*

### The ruled

Life for the people of the Bantustans was tough. Their lot was poverty, disease and malnutrition. In the midst of a country whose white population enjoyed one of the highest standards of living in the world, they lived in the same style as people in the poorest countries in the world. They were overcrowded, so land could not be farmed efficiently. This became worse over time as more and more black people were forced to move from white areas. Blacks whose labour was no longer needed in white South Africa were sent to the Bantustans. Between 1960 and 1980:

- 1,129,000 black people were removed from white farms, where they had been tenants or labourers. Greater use of machines meant that the farmers did not need their labour any more
- 1,616,000 were removed from urban areas, mostly under the Group Areas Act. People found themselves moved hundreds of kilometres from their homes, to open patches of infertile land.

**S**OURCE 7   The gambling tables at Sun City, where blacks and whites mixed in ways forbidden in white-controlled South Africa

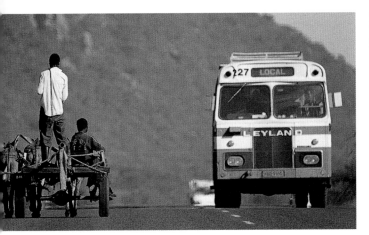

**SOURCE 8** A bus transporting people from a Bantustan to the city to work

**SOURCE 9** Evidence from the Surplus Peoples Project, based at Cape Town University, about a forced removal from Port Elizabeth to Glenmore, 200 km away

*" The trucks came very early when they were asleep. The officials were angry men who shouted at them to get out. The houses were demolished before they could get their belongings out. Their furniture was broken.*

*The houses they were taken to in Glenmore were bare, with draughty wooden walls they had to fix with mud. Tsotsobe looks at us and says that now there is no hope. When he was young he wanted to give his children and grandchildren a different kind of life. Now he sees that there is no hope for his children. "*

**SOURCE 10** These homes for people forcibly removed to Welcome Valley in 1968 consisted only of toilet blocks. The rest of the housing was not yet built

The only way to stay alive was to find work, and the only work was in white South Africa. Many 'residents' of the Bantustans actually worked away. For some this meant a precarious life dodging the Pass Laws in a city, living in an illegal squatter camp. For others, it meant travelling long distances from their homes in the Bantustan to offices or factories in white areas. Some travelled for six hours every day by bus. Huge townships sprang up in parts of Bantustans close to white urban areas: Botshabelo, for example, grew from 100,000 in 1980 to 300,000 in 1985. Hundreds of buses carried the people 50 km to work in Bloemfontein each day.

The creation of the Bantustans made life even more difficult for black people living in the towns and cities. They now faced the constant threat of removal to a 'homeland'.

**SOURCE 11** Knocking down the Crossroads squatter camp at Cape Flats, near Cape Town, in 1986

Nervously they walked up the drive to the big front door. Before they dared to knock they heard a fierce barking from inside which made them grip each other's hands, ready to run back to the street. Then they heard a sharp voice inside call out, in English:

'Joyce, see who it is.'

The door opened ...

As Mma gasped, the children flung themselves at her and she clasped them in her arms, hugging them. Tears welled up in her eyes as the children sobbed against her.

'What is wrong?' Mma cried softly.

'Who is it, Joyce?' came a brisk voice from behind.

Mma stifled her sobs.

'Madam, these are my children.'

'What are they doing here?' asked the white lady.

'Madam, I don't know. They haven't told me yet.'

'Dineo is very ill, Mma,' Naledi said, 'Her fever won't go away. Tiro and I have come to bring you home.'

Mma gasped again and held her children more tightly.

'Madam, my little girl is very sick. Can I go home to see her?'

The Madam raised her eyebrows.

'Well, Joyce, I can't possibly let you go today. I need you tonight. The Master and I are having an important dinner party. But I suppose you can go tomorrow.'

'Thank you, Madam.'

'I hope you realise how inconvenient this is for me. If you are not back in a week, I shall just have to look for another maid, you understand?'

'Yes, Madam.'

The children couldn't follow everything the Madam was saying in English, but her voice sounded annoyed, while Mma spoke so softly. The children huddled close to Mma's starched white apron. They hadn't seen her in this strange servant's uniform before. As Mma led the children through to the kitchen, they glanced across at open doors leading to other large rooms. A wide staircase led upwards. Never had they imagined a house could be this size.

In the kitchen Mma gave them a drink of water and some porridge she had cooked earlier. Naledi noticed that Mma took the tin plates and mugs for them from a separate little cupboard.

**S**OURCE 12 An extract from a children's book called *Journey to Jo'burg*, by Beverley Naidoo. It tells how two children, Naledi and her younger brother Tiro, live with their aunt on a reservation with their baby sister Dineo. Their mother ('Mma' in Tswana, their language) works as a maid almost 500 km away in Johannesburg. Dineo is ill, so the children decide to go and tell their mother. After several adventures they arrive outside the big house in the white suburb where their mother works

1. Why couldn't the mother live with her children?
2. What did the children find surprising about the house where their mother worked?
3. In what ways did the Mistress have power over their mother?
4. Why did they eat and drink from separate utensils?
5. What else does this part of the story tell you about apartheid?
6. This source is fiction. What is its value as evidence about South Africa at this time?

Verwoerd was absolutely certain that his policies were right. As the rest of the world condemned him, he stood up to them. The whites appreciated him for that, and for keeping white supremacy and prosperity intact. He might have ruled South Africa for many more years but was assassinated in 1966 by a mentally disturbed white man. He was succeeded as Prime Minister by John Vorster, an enthusiastic supporter of Verwoerd's vision of apartheid.

■ **TASK**

In Source 2 at the beginning of this enquiry Verwoerd said: 'If South Africa has to choose between being poor and white or rich and multiracial, then it must choose to be white.' Look back over the section on the Bantustans (pages 54–58).

1. By introducing the Bantustan policy, how did the government try to:
a) make South Africa all-white?
b) keep white South Africans rich?
2. In what ways did the Bantustan policy cost South Africa money?
3. 'Despite making comments like the one in the quote above, Verwoerd in fact tried to make South Africa white *and* rich.' Use your answers to questions 1 and 2 and any other evidence you have to comment on the truth of this statement.

# What impact did apartheid have on the lives of South Africans?

IN THIS CHAPTER you have found out about the setting up and development of apartheid. You have looked at the laws and at what the politicians were trying to do. But what effect did apartheid have on the lives of South Africans, both blacks and whites?

On the following three pages you will meet six families. Their stories are invented but they are closely based on real people. The year is 1976.

## ■ TASK

As you read about them, think about the following:

■ which family has the best life?
■ which has the worst?
■ which person do you think would be the happiest?
■ who do you think would be the most angry?
■ which family would you most like to visit? Why?

## The whites

**David Barclay.** Aged 45. English-speaking. White business executive with a British firm. He earns R70,000 a year. Been in South Africa since his parents emigrated there from Britain in 1947. Enjoys a prosperous lifestyle. Mr Barclay supports the United Party. He does not see an all-white future for South Africa as realistic. He wants to see apartheid's tougher laws removed so that blacks can get educated and move to cities and look for jobs on the same basis as whites. He is not politically active, and has one black friend among his circle, a journalist on the *Rand Daily Mail*, the newspaper which he reads. He owns a Mercedes. He visits Europe frequently.

**Elizabeth Barclay.** Aged 40, is well-educated (University of London), has lived in South Africa only since her marriage. Supports the Liberal Party and is a moderately active member of the 'Black Sash' organisation (see page 72). She tries to be friendly towards the Barclay's 'maid', Lucy, giving her presents for her family, feeding and paying her well, and tolerating the occasional visits of her boyfriend to her rooms.

The Barclays have two children, both boys, aged twelve and ten, who attend all-white, fee-paying schools.

**Hendrick De Kok** is an ex-miner, aged 53, no longer able to work because he has phthisis, the miners' lung disease. He is Afrikaans-speaking, a supporter of the National Party and of apartheid. Born on his father's farm, he moved to Johannesburg at the age of 18. The De Koks live in their own bungalow in a white housing area east of Johannesburg. He has a reasonably good disability pension and they can afford a second-hand car. Mr De Kok cannot get about much, but he attends the local Dutch Reformed Church every Sunday, as well as occasional meetings of his all-white Miners Union branch, of which he used to be secretary. Since the government finally gave in and allowed TV into South Africa in 1976 Mr De Kok spends much of his time watching sport, of which he is a keen follower.

**Mrs De Kok** is a keen supporter of their Dutch Reformed Church, which takes up most of her leisure time. She also looks after her grandchildren from time to time. The De Koks have two daughters, both in their thirties: one is married to a railway clerk and works part-time; one is married to a policeman.

## The Indians

**Ama Naidoo.** She is 40 years old and lives in a small house in the Indian housing area. She is a strict Hindu and lives off her earnings from a tiny flower stall she operates near the centre of Johannesburg. She has to spend almost all her waking hours at work. She is married to **James Naidoo**, a carpenter, and has a daughter, aged eight, who is looked after by her mother and father who live nearby. She carries on the interest in politics she shares with her husband. Until it was banned she was a member of the ANC. As a young woman she took part in women's anti-pass demonstrations in the 1950s.

## The black Africans

**Michael Nkosana.** Aged 37. A successful Xhosa-speaking businessman. He operates a fleet of 30 'combis', the minibuses which, starting at 4.30 a.m., ferry black workers from the townships into central and white areas of Johannesburg, so that they are there in time to make breakfast for white households. He was educated at an Anglican mission school. He belongs to a stokval, a system in which blacks with a little money lend it in turn to each other to help their businesses. This enables them to make capital expenditure (like buying more minibuses) without having to rely on white-controlled banks. He lives in a four-bedroom house in the prosperous part of Soweto. He loathes petty apartheid and the white privileges which prevent him from being able to get on as rapidly as a white businessman might. He resents having to carry his pass all the time and be talked down to by ignorant young white police. However, he is not politically active; his combi company relies on government subsidies to keep fares down and that means he has to keep on the right side of the authorities.

**Nomsa Nkosana.** Aged 38. Wife of Michael. She is one of the few women in Soweto who is wealthy enough not to have to work. She is an active member of her local church, the Methodist Episcopal Church, and organises social events in connection with the church. She also holds social events for other better-off black wives in her part of Soweto.

**Abel and Amry Nkosana.** Aged 16 and 14. Into reggae and black US music. Abel plays and watches football. Deeply contemptuous of apartheid and their parents' apparent acceptance of it.

**Thabo Zondo.** Aged 29, he is a Zulu and a mineworker. He lives in a compound along with 150 other Zulu mineworkers. He works 1.5 km underground, as a skilled driller. He works six days a week for nine months, then returns to his home and family in the Zulu homeland of KwaZulu. His life is one longing for the end of his work session.

**Mary Zondo.** Aged 31, she is married to Thabo. They have six children and live in poverty on a tiny patch of dry, scrubby land in KwaZulu. She has to look after the children, walk 3 km each day for water, and walk even further sometimes to gather sticks for fuel to cook with. She tends the crops and the two scrawny cows they own. Without Thabo's money they could not possibly survive and she waits longingly for his return. They then have six to eight weeks together before he has to go back to the mine compound.

**Dikeledi Setshedi.** Aged 35, a Sotho. She lives in an unofficial settlement outside Johannesburg. Her house, built of breeze blocks by her and the man who was living with her four years ago, is better than most. Most are made of only corrugated iron or hammered petrol cans. Dikeledi is a shebeen queen: that is, she makes a living making skokiaan, or African beer, although this is illegal in the townships. She had a child when she was 17 and so had to give up her job as a maid to look after him. She regards paying fines, police bribes and pay-offs to gangsters as just part of life. Her shebeen is popular at the moment as her man is a jazz musician and people flock to listen and to drink.

**Mokete Setshedi.** Aged 40. Dikeledi's sister. Makes a living taking in washing from white households and helping her sister.

**Joseph Setshedi.** Now aged 18 and a member of a street gang – a tsotsi. He lives off petty thieving and is a snappy dresser.

**Thomas Setshedi.** Aged 13. Half-brother to Joseph. Helps his mother with the brewing and his aunt with the washing, but wants to get educated and move out. He makes a few pennies selling sweets to blacks returning to the township in the evening. He refuses to join the dangerous life and probable early death of his half-brother. Has read some Black Consciousness leaflets (see page 83) and is excited by them.

## ■ TASK

How did apartheid affect these six families? On your own copy of this table, make notes about the six aspects of apartheid we have looked at in this chapter and their effects on these families. (Note: You may not find anything to write in some boxes.) Is there anyone totally unaffected by apartheid? Who is affected most?

|  | Defining people by race | Separating people in public places | Separating housing areas | Educating children separately | Dividing the country into separate areas | Crushing opposition |
|---|---|---|---|---|---|---|
| The Barclays |  |  |  |  |  |  |
| The De Koks |  |  |  |  |  |  |
| The Naidoos |  |  |  |  |  |  |
| The Nkosanas |  |  |  |  |  |  |
| The Zondos |  |  |  |  |  |  |
| The Setshedis |  |  |  |  |  |  |

## ■ ACTIVITY

Choose one of the families in this enquiry. It is Friday evening. The family members have met together and are talking about the weekend ahead. The conversation moves on to talk about independence for Transkei and KwaZulu, due to take place in 1976. Is the Bantustan policy a good idea? Will it change their lives? In what ways? Write a script for the conversation that might take place.

# **W**as apartheid bound to fail?

**I**N ORDER TO answer this question, you need to know whether there were problems that the apartheid system could not overcome. Although apartheid seemed safe and secure in the late 1970s, there *were* problems ahead. In the end these problems led to its collapse. Look at the sources below and opposite, and decide how each one presented a problem for apartheid.

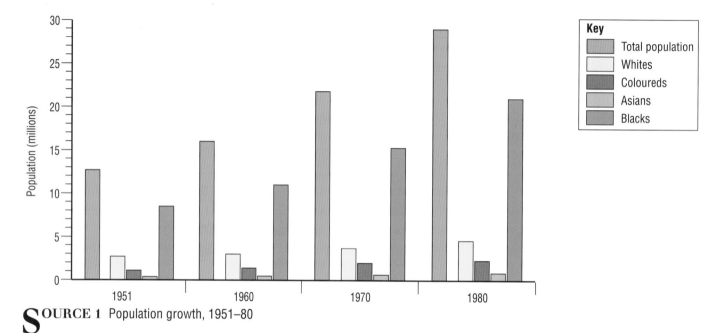

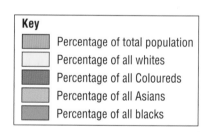

**S**OURCE 1 Population growth, 1951–80

1. How have the numbers of black Africans increased over 30 years?
2. How have the proportions of whites and non-whites changed over the 30 years?
3. How would both of these facts present difficulties for apartheid?

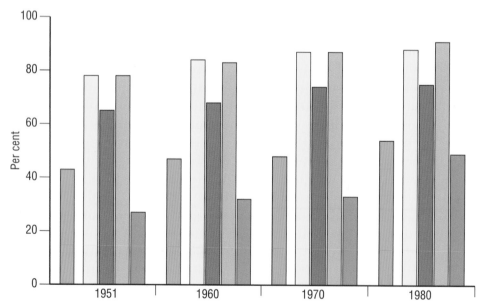

**S**OURCE 2 Proportion of the population living in urban areas, 1951–80

4. How has the percentage of black Africans in urban areas changed?
5. How does this show that apartheid was not working?

| | Whites | Coloureds | Asians | Blacks |
|---|---|---|---|---|
| Average monthly household income in rands in 1985 | 1,958 | 680 | 1,109 | 352 |
| Infant deaths per 1,000 live births, 1988 | 9 | 41 | 14 | 62 |
| Life expectancy, 1988 | 72 | 62 | 67 | 60 |
| Incidence of tuberculosis per 100,000 population, 1987 | 16 | 532 | 53 | 164 |

**S**OURCE 3  Income, health and life expectancy in the 1980s

6. What do these figures tell us about the inequality of apartheid?
7. What are the links between the figures?
8. How do you think these statistics present a problem for the supporters of apartheid?

| | Britain | South Africa |
|---|---|---|
| Murders | 1 | 27 |
| Rapes | NO FIGURES | 63 |
| Robberies | 27 | 178 |
| Assaults | 176 | 1,328 |

**S**OURCE 4  A comparison of crime rates in Britain and South Africa per 100,000 people, 1979

9. Suggest reasons for the differences between Britain and South Africa in these figures.
10. Apart from the figures in Sources 1–4, what else would you want to know about South Africa to help you decide whether the apartheid idea was bound to fail?

## ■ TASK 1

'Complete separation of the races was bound to fail.' Use Sources 1–4 and the other information in this chapter to comment on how accurate you think this statement is. Your teacher will give you a sheet to help you plan your answer.

## ■ TASK 2

In this chapter we have found out that apartheid set out to:

1. define which race every person belonged to and prevent any more people of mixed race being born
2. separate the races in public places
3. separate the areas where different races lived
4. separate the races in schools
5. divide the whole country into different areas for whites and blacks and exclude blacks from white areas as far as possible
6. crush opposition from anyone who opposed these plans.

Copy and complete this table to make a summary of the main apartheid policies and their effects.

| Policy | Act(s) setting it up, with date | Results |
|---|---|---|
| 1 | | |
| 2 | | |
| 3 | | |
| 4 | | |
| 5 | | |
| 6 | | |

## ■ TASK 3

We also looked at some of the questions historians ask about apartheid. On a copy of this table note down a brief summary answer to each question.

| Question | My summary answer |
|---|---|
| Was there anything new about apartheid? | |
| Was apartheid all planned from the start? | |
| How did apartheid change under Verwoerd? | |
| Was apartheid bound to fail? | |

# chapter 5

# HOW DID BLACK SOUTH AFRICAN RESISTANCE TO APARTHEID CHANGE BETWEEN 1948 AND 1976?

## Introduction

APARTHEID HAD MADE the situation of black men, women and children worse. In jobs, housing, family life, schools, personal freedom, in little ways and big, life-threatening ways, black South Africans felt under pressure. Should they just knuckle under and accept things? How could they resist?

**SOURCE 1** An extract from a speech by Nelson Mandela in 1948

*❝ In their homes and local areas, in provincial and national gatherings, on trains and buses, in factories and on the farms, in cities, shantytowns, schools and prisons, the African people have discussed the shameful misdeeds of those who rule the country.*

*Year after year they have raised their voices in condemnation of the grinding poverty, the low wages, the acute shortage of land, the inhuman exploitation and the whole policy of white domination. But instead of more freedom, repression grows in volume and intensity. ❞*

### ■ TALKING POINT

Sources 1 and 2 show the negative side. What about the positive side? What power did black South Africans have? Think about the kinds of protest that black people had made already. Suggest two or three ways in which they could take action to resist apartheid.

We have almost no civil rights. We don't have the vote, nor the right to organise protests. We can't speak freely, nor publish our views.

I live in a squatter camp on the edge of Johannesburg. My cousin works on a farm in Transkei. The problems we face are very different.

Just living from day to day is hard enough. We don't have any time or energy left for politics.

There's no group that can speak for all of us. If we do try to resist, who will lead us?

Most of us have had very little education.

I don't want to work with the Coloureds and Asians. I prefer to stick with my own people, the Zulus.

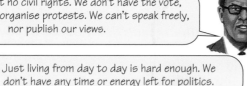

If we protest we'll probably get arrested or sent into exile. The police seem to get away with anything.

**SOURCE 2** Factors that made it difficult for black South Africans to resist apartheid

**SOURCE 3** A cartoon from a newspaper which was critical of the National Party, 1950

### ■ TASK 1

1. Look at the difficulties black South Africans speak of on the opposite page. Which of these do you think was the most serious?
2. Which of these difficulties could blacks do something about?
3. What do Sources 3 and 5 suggest is the strength of the black South African people?
4. How could this strength be turned into action?
5. How do actions like the one announced in Source 6 make use of this strength?

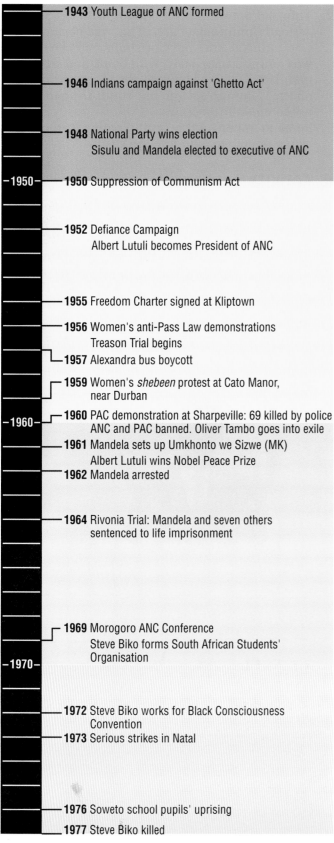

**1943** Youth League of ANC formed

**1946** Indians campaign against 'Ghetto Act'

**1948** National Party wins election
Sisulu and Mandela elected to executive of ANC

—1950— **1950** Suppression of Communism Act

**1952** Defiance Campaign
Albert Lutuli becomes President of ANC

**1955** Freedom Charter signed at Kliptown

**1956** Women's anti-Pass Law demonstrations
Treason Trial begins
**1957** Alexandra bus boycott

**1959** Women's *shebeen* protest at Cato Manor,
near Durban

—1960— **1960** PAC demonstration at Sharpeville: 69 killed by police
ANC and PAC banned. Oliver Tambo goes into exile
**1961** Mandela sets up Umkhonto we Sizwe (MK)
Albert Lutuli wins Nobel Peace Prize
**1962** Mandela arrested

**1964** Rivonia Trial: Mandela and seven others
sentenced to life imprisonment

**1969** Morogoro ANC Conference
Steve Biko forms South African Students'
Organisation

—1970—

**1972** Steve Biko works for Black Consciousness
Convention
**1973** Serious strikes in Natal

**1976** Soweto school pupils' uprising
**1977** Steve Biko killed

**S**OURCE 4  A timeline showing black resistance, 1943–77

**S**OURCE 5  A cartoon from a South African newspaper which opposed apartheid, 1948

## NATIONAL DAY OF PROTEST

Monday 26th June, 1950

### DO NOT GO TO WORK ON THIS DAY

<u>Defeat</u> the laws turning our country into a police state!

Don't allow government laws to crush our liberty!

Fight for freedom!

Votes and a decent wage for all!

**S**OURCE 6  A poster from June 1950

## ■ TASK 2

Resistance to apartheid took many forms over the 28 years dealt with in this chapter. The timeline in Source 4 gives you an outline of the main protests. To help you see the different patterns, on your own copy:

1. underline with a single line protests involving the ANC
2. underline with a double line protests involving women
3. underline with a dotted line protests involving Black Consciousness
4. underline with a wavy line trade union protests.

# How did the ANC become an active resistance organisation?

ONE DAY IN 1941 a tall, impressive, young black man stepped out of a train at Johannesburg station. He emerged into the streets of a city full of prosperity for its white population, full of violence and poverty for its blacks. Up to then he had lived only in rural South Africa, in Transkei. He had been educated and privileged. Now he was running away; running away from a secure future as a chief, and the wife his guardian had found for him; running away from college, where he had joined in protests. His name was Nelson Mandela and he was 22 years old. These were times of great change in his country and he wanted to take part in those changes. It was a journey that was to take him, via 26 years in prison, to the Presidency of the first multiracial government of South Africa.

## The foundation of the Youth League

Mandela met up with Walter Sisulu, an older man and a Christian, who gave him a job as a lawyer's clerk. He was joined by his friend Oliver Tambo, a brilliant student who was thinking of becoming a priest. Tambo joined Mandela when he opened the first all-black law firm in South Africa in 1952. Mandela was keen on keeping fit and did some boxing. The three friends spent all their spare time discussing what black people had to do to win equal rights in their own country. They were joined in their discussions by a dynamic young ex-teacher, Anton Lembede. Lembede was an AFRICANIST, that is, he believed Africans should throw off feelings of inferiority towards whites. They had to win their freedom by themselves, not in co-operation with non-Africans such as whites and Indians.

Sisulu was a member of the African National Congress, the ANC (see pages 33–34). Lembede criticised the ANC for trying to win the respect of whites by their good behaviour. He called them 'a body of gentlemen with clean hands'. However, Sisulu persuaded his friends to join. Together, they formed the Youth League in 1943 to inject some life into the ANC. Lembede actually became Youth League President.

The Youth League had the following views.

1. They did not want to co-operate with the Indian National Congress, which was campaigning for Indians in South Africa. This was because they saw Indians as non-Africans, with different problems.

2. They did not want to co-operate with the South African Communist Party. This was because Communists were not Christians and because it was a multiracial party, with black and white members. Nelson Mandela wrote savage attacks on the Communists and the Youth League even broke up their meetings.

3. Some members of the Youth League wanted to 'drive the white man into the sea'.

## ■ ACTIVITY

You are a young black South African from Cape Town who is visiting the ANC Youth League in Johannesburg. It is 1944 and Anton Lembede, Nelson Mandela, Walter Sisulu and Oliver Tambo are present, as well as others. You have been asked by your friends back home to get answers to three important questions.

Should we work with the Coloured people of the Cape who are also suffering under apartheid?

Should we work with whites who are opposed to apartheid?

Should we work with the Communist Party of South Africa which is also opposed to apartheid?

Read through the next section. What answers do the members of the Youth League give you? (You might get different answers from different people.)

SOURCE 1 A speech by Anton Lembede to an ANC conference

❝ Look at my skin, it is black, black like the soil of Mother Africa. We must believe that we are inferior to no other race. We must develop race pride. ❞

## The Programme of Action

In 1947 Lembede died. Mandela and Tambo took over the Youth League and planned a Programme of Action:

■ to reject racial segregation completely
■ to work independently of whites
■ to take non-violent action: boycotts, strikes, civil disobedience.

**SOURCE 2** An extract from a Youth League document, 1947

*66 A condition for inter-racial peace and progress is the abandonment of white domination ... Our goal is the winning of national freedom for African people and a people's free society where racial persecution and oppression will be outlawed. 99*

In 1948, just as the Nationalists were beginning to set up apartheid, and despite the opposition of the older leaders, they pushed the Programme of Action through the ANC. Several Youth League members, including Mandela, were elected to the ANC Executive. Walter Sisulu became Secretary, on a salary of £5 a month (his wife, Albertina, a nurse, kept them alive on her wages).

These were the anxious, restless years just after the end of the Second World War. Nelson Mandela and other members of the Youth League were excited at the prospect of equality held out by the Charter of the United Nations, set up in 1945. They were encouraged when India became independent in 1947. On the other hand, there seemed little hope of change in South Africa. White opinion was moving in the opposite way, if anything. The election of the Nationalist government in 1948 (see page 32) was alarming. The beginning of apartheid seemed to push black people further away from gaining equal rights.

Mandela also began to realise that he had a lot to learn from both the Indians and the Communists. The Indian National Congress, founded by Gandhi, was committed to non-violence. In 1946 they were involved in a campaign against the 'Ghetto Act' (see page 38). Mandela saw that their problems were not that different from those of black Africans and he was impressed by their non-violent tactics. Soon he was working alongside the Indian National Congress.

He also learnt from seeing the Communist Party organise massive support among striking workers on 1 May 1950. He could see the power of mass support and knew that the ANC did not yet have that kind of strength.

**SOURCE 3** Yusuf Dadoo, Indian National Congress leader, speaking to a crowd in Johannesburg in 1945. Nelson Mandela is standing just behind the microphone

## The Defiance Campaign, 1952

**SOURCE 4** A letter from the ANC to the Prime Minister in April 1952 explaining why they are starting the Defiance Campaign

*66 We would point out that as a defenceless and voteless people, we have explored other channels without success. The African people are left with no other alternative. We desire to state that it is our intention to conduct this campaign in a peaceful manner and that any disturbances, if they do occur, will not be of our making. 99*

The new leaders of the ANC planned a campaign of defiance of apartheid. Mandela was put in charge. He called for 10,000 volunteers: 8,577 responded. On 6 April 1952, as whites celebrated 300 years since the arrival of the Dutch, ANC supporters all over South Africa defied the apartheid regulations. They got into 'whites only' compartments of trains, they queued at 'whites only' counters at post offices, they sat on 'whites only' benches. They were arrested in thousands. 'Open the jail doors, we want to enter!' they shouted. By October 2,354 people had been arrested. The courts were clogged by their numbers and, just as they had hoped, the newspapers, in South Africa and abroad, were full of their exploits.

ANC membership rose from about 7,000 to 100,000. It was on its way to becoming the voice of black resistance.

**S**OURCE 5 The Defiance Campaign: these people were protesting about apartheid laws at Berea Station in Durban by occupying the 'Europeans Only' waiting room

## ■ TALKING POINTS

1. Why was it important for Nelson Mandela to get thousands of volunteers for the Defiance Campaign?
2. Why was it important to be non-violent?
3. Do you think the non-violence campaign is going to work?

## ■ TASK 1

Write a short essay about Nelson Mandela's political career from 1941 to 1952. The question to explore is: 'What does Nelson Mandela's political career tell us about the ways black resistance was changing in the years 1941–52?'
This is how you are going to do it:

1. For each of the following turning-points in his life during these years, write a sentence describing **what happened**.
2. Then explain, in two or three sentences, **how this event changed Mandela's ideas**.
3. End with a short paragraph explaining in your own words **how black resistance through the ANC had changed** in these years.

   ■ Arrives in Johannesburg, 1941
   ■ Joins Youth League of ANC, 1943
   ■ Works with Indian National Congress, 1946
   ■ Joins Executive of ANC, 1948
   ■ Sees Communist Party active in Johannesburg, 1950
   ■ Organises Defiance Campaign, 1952

## The Freedom Charter

The next move, the ANC decided, was to call a nationwide meeting, a Congress. It would bring together delegates from all the organisations that the ANC had learnt to work with: trade unions, Coloured people, the Indian Congress and some whites. ANC volunteers went out to ask people what their demands were. These demands were listed in a Freedom Charter. The organisers could therefore claim that it contained what the people of South Africa wanted.

**S**OURCE 6 The Congress Alliance called on people to send in their grievances and their ideas for the kind of South Africa they wanted

*66 WE CALL THE FARMERS OF THE RESERVES AND TRUST LANDS!*

*Let us speak of the wide lands and the narrow strips on which we toil. Let us speak of the brothers without land and the children without schooling. Let us speak of taxes and of cattle and of famine.*

*LET US SPEAK OF FREEDOM!*
*WE CALL THE MINERS OF COAL, GOLD AND DIAMONDS!*

*Let us speak of the dark shafts and the cold compounds far from our families. 99*

4. What does Source 6 tell you about how the organisers tried to appeal to the ordinary working people of South Africa?

**S**OURCE 7 An organiser describes going out into the countryside to collect demands

*66 We got resolutions from women, farmworkers, the whole lot. We even got resolutions written on the back of cigarette boxes, pieces of cardboard or paper. It was a difficult task because people were not used to expressing themselves openly. The volunteer had to explain carefully: 'Look, I'm not telling you what to say, you tell me what you want.' Demands varied from being unable to get a uniform at work, or for wives to be able to live with their husbands, to much more political ideas such as votes for all. 99*

5. According to Source 7, what problems did the organisers have in drawing up the Charter?

**S**OURCE 8 Some of the crowd at the Congress held at Kliptown on 26 June 1955, when the Freedom Charter was agreed

The Charter Congress met at Kliptown outside Johannesburg, on 26 June 1955. Most of their leaders were under arrest, or banned from attending political meetings. The crowd was surrounded by police. Walter Sisulu and Nelson Mandela, both 'banned', watched the proceedings in secret. Despite the difficulties, nearly 3,000 delegates managed to get to the meeting: 320 Indians, 230 Coloureds, 112 whites and 2,200 black South Africans. The organisers claimed that it was the first really democratic assembly in South Africa's history.

The Freedom Charter (see page 70) was read out and the crowd greeted and agreed each point by calling out 'Africa!' or '*Mayibuye*' (which means 'Let us return'). At the end, they all sang 'Nkosi Sikelel' iAfrika' ('God bless Africa'). Mandela called it 'a spectacular and moving demonstration'. The Charter gave the ANC a manifesto – a clear statement of their demands. They could claim, with some justice, that the Charter had popular support. It became the basis of their campaigning right up to the 1994 election.

### ■ TALKING POINT

'The Freedom Charter gave the ANC a manifesto – a clear statement of their demands.' How had the ANC moved on from what it was like when Anton Lembede called it 'a body of gentlemen with clean hands'?

### ■ TASK 2

Look at the 10 points in Source 9 on page 70.

| Democratic | Socialist | Welfare | Freedom |
|---|---|---|---|
|  |  |  |  |
|  |  |  |  |
|  |  |  |  |

1. Place each of the points in one – or more – of the columns on a copy of this table. Discuss your decisions with someone else.
2. Nelson Mandela, on trial for his life in 1964, claimed that the Charter was 'not a blueprint for SOCIALISM'. Was this a fair claim?

### ■ TASK 3

1. Look at Sources 6 and 7 and Source 9. Do you think the Freedom Charter really was what ordinary South Africans wanted?
2. 'South Africa belongs to all who live in it' and 'All national groups shall have equal rights'. Why might an Africanist disagree?
3. What do you think a white supporter of apartheid would say about the Charter?

*We, the people of South Africa, declare for all our country and the world to know:*

*That South Africa belongs to all who live in it, black and white, and that no government can justly claim authority unless it is based on the will of the people.*

*That our people have been robbed of their birthright to land, liberty and peace by a form of government founded on injustice and inequality.*

*That our country will never be prosperous or free until all our people live in brotherhood, enjoying equal rights and opportunities.*

*That only a democratic state, based on the will of the people, can secure to all their birthright, without distinction of colour, race, sex or belief.*

*And therefore, we, the people of South Africa, black and white together – equals, countrymen and brothers – adopt this FREEDOM CHARTER. And we pledge ourselves to strive together, sparing nothing of our strength and courage, until the democratic changes here set out have been won.*

1. **THE PEOPLE SHALL GOVERN**
   (One person one vote.)

2. **ALL NATIONAL GROUPS SHALL HAVE EQUAL RIGHTS**
   (An end to apartheid.)

3. **ALL PEOPLE SHALL SHARE IN THE NATION'S WEALTH**
   (The wealth of South Africa, its minerals, banks and industries, shall belong to the people.)

4. **THE LAND SHALL BE SHARED BY THOSE WHO WORK IT**
   (The land shall be re-divided among all farmers, whatever their race.)

5. **ALL SHALL BE EQUAL BEFORE THE LAW**
   (Fair trials and an end to banning orders.)

6. **ALL SHALL ENJOY HUMAN RIGHTS**
   (Everyone should have the right to speak, organise, meet, publish, preach, worship, educate their children freely. Pass Laws shall be abolished.)

7. **THERE SHALL BE WORK AND SECURITY**
   (Trade unions shall be recognised. Equal pay for equal work for men and women of all races. Sick leave for all workers and maternity pay for mothers.)

8. **THE DOORS OF LEARNING AND CULTURE SHALL BE OPENED**
   (Education shall be free, compulsory and equal for all children.)

9. **THERE SHALL BE HOUSES, SECURITY AND COMFORT**
   (Rents and prices lowered, food for all, free medical care, slums demolished, elderly, orphans, disabled and sick to be cared for by the government.)

10. **LET THERE BE PEACE AND FRIENDSHIP**
    (South Africa will respect the independence of all nations and seek to resolve disputes by negotiation not war.)

THESE FREEDOMS WE WILL FIGHT FOR, SIDE BY SIDE, THROUGHOUT OUR LIVES, UNTIL WE HAVE WON OUR LIBERTY!

**S**OURCE 9 The opening words of the Freedom Charter and its main points (**NOTE**: These have been summarised for this book and are not numbered in the original document)

# What other forms did resistance to apartheid take in the 1950s?

## ACTIVITY

You are a British TV reporter in South Africa. It is late 1959 and your editor has asked you for a piece about opposition to apartheid during the 1950s. Use the information on the following three pages to write notes for the programme you will make.

The programme will have three sections:

a) women's protests
b) bus boycotts
c) rural protests.

For each protest you have covered over the last ten years, note down your thoughts under the headings:

- motives
- methods
- aims
- results.

End with a short piece summing up how resistance to apartheid has changed between 1950 and 1959.

BETWEEN 1948 AND 1960 the ANC organised some powerful protests against apartheid. It was widely respected abroad (Chief Albert Lutuli, President of the ANC from 1952, was awarded the Nobel Peace Prize in 1961). It had increased its following inside South Africa. But ANC protests were not the only ones to take place in these years. South African men and women were driven to take action on their own.

SOURCE 1 Albert Lutuli

SOURCE 2 Albert Lutuli, President of the ANC, speaking in 1958

66 *I sometimes wonder if life is not a series of surprises for the National Party. Most of them perhaps really do think that Africans are so thick-skinned and limited in understanding that they would not notice things like malnutrition, low wages, leaking roofs, police brutality, unless an 'agitator' came to point it out. It takes them aback when we arrive at our own conclusions and resolve to do something about them.* 99

1. Why, according to Lutuli, must life be a 'series of surprises' to Nationalists?
2. What does Lutuli say about:
   a) what the Nationalists think of the blacks?
   b) what they think of the causes of black protests?
3. What, according to Lutuli, are the real causes?

## Women and protest

SOURCE 3 A statement by Vukani Makhosikazi, from the book *South African Women Speak*, edited by Ingrid Obery

66 *We women share with our menfolk the cares and anxieties imposed by poverty and its evils. As wives and mothers, it falls upon us to make small wages stretch a long way. It is we who feel the cries of our children when they are hungry and sick. It is our lot to keep and care for the homes that are too small, broken and dirty to be kept clean. We know the burden of looking after children and land when our husbands are away in the mines, on the farms, earning our daily bread.*

*We know what it is to keep the family life going in shanties or crowded one-room apartments. We know the bitterness of the children taking up lawless ways, of daughters becoming unmarried mothers while still at school.* 99

## TASK

1. In what ways does apartheid hit women differently from men, according to Source 3?
2. 'Apartheid hit women harder than men.' Use the family histories on pages 59–61 as well as in this chapter to find evidence both to support and to contradict this statement. When you have enough evidence, decide whether men or women suffered most and explain your decision.

### Anti-Pass Law demonstrations

From 1952, the government decided to extend the hated Pass Law system to women. Peaceful demonstrations were held in many parts of South Africa. In Johannesburg, Albertina Sisulu led the demonstrators and was imprisoned and banned. (At one point, in 1963, she was in prison, her husband, Walter, was banned and on the run from the police, and their teenage son was also under arrest. The rest of their children were looked after by a fourteen-year-old cousin.)

In 1956 a group of women of all races asked to meet the government minister responsible for the Pass Laws to discuss their effects. He refused even to reply and so a massive all-women demonstration occupied government offices in Pretoria.

**S**OURCE 4 Helen Joseph describes the anti-pass demonstration of August 1956 when thousands of women entered government offices in Pretoria

  **❝** *Four women had been chosen as leaders for the day: Lilian Ngoyi, the African; Rahima Moosa, the Indian; Sophie Williams, the Coloured; and I, the white. We took the piles of protests and left them outside ministers' offices when our knocking brought no response: 'We have not come here to plead but to ask for what is our right as mothers, as women and as citizens of this country . . .'*

  *Lilian Ngoyi asked them all to stand in silent protest. As she raised her arm in the Congress salute, 20,000 arms went up and stayed there those endless minutes. We knew that all over South Africa women in cities and towns were gathered in protest . . .*

  *At the end of half an hour Lilian began to sing, softly at first 'Nkosi Sikelel' iAfrika'. For the blacks it has become their anthem and the voices rose, louder and louder. Then I heard a new song, composed especially for the protest 'Wathint' a bafazi, wa uthint' imbolodo uso kufa.' ['You have struck a rock, you have tampered with the women, you shall be destroyed.']* **❞**

## ■ TALKING POINT

The women's anti-Pass Laws demonstration did not stop the introduction of passes for women. Does that mean these demonstrations were wasted? Discuss your answers.

### The Black Sash

This organisation of white, mainly middle-class women worked to help black women in difficulties over the Pass Laws and other apartheid restrictions.

**S**OURCE 5 Women from the Black Sash demonstrating against the Pass Laws, 1955

### Beer-hall protests

One of the few ways a black woman in a city could make an independent living was to brew beer and sell it in a *shebeen* – a kind of beer-hall – in her own home (see page 61). This was a traditional way for women to contribute to African social life, but it was banned by the government, who built official beer-halls. Police raided the *shebeens* and women were often fined heavily. In Cato Manor, near Durban in 1959, women became so annoyed by police harassment of their *shebeens* that they attacked and burnt two official beer-halls. The next day they were themselves violently attacked by the police.

**S**OURCE 6 Police attack a women's march protesting about closing down their *shebeens* (beer-halls) at Cato Manor, near Durban, in 1959

## Bus boycotts

One result of the apartheid laws that controlled where people could live (the Group Areas Act of 1950 and the Native Resettlement Act of 1954) was that Africans were driven from homes near the centres of cities, out into townships many kilometres away. Yet their jobs were still in the city centres and white suburbs. They could not afford cars, so they were utterly dependent on buses.

  The government actually paid the bus companies money to keep fares down (this stopped people asking for higher wages). Some bus companies nevertheless did put up fares. This caused great unrest and hardship. In 1957 in the township of Alexandra, 16 km from Johannesburg, people boycotted the buses. This meant they faced a round trip of 32 km, walking all the way. The police harassed them and accused the ANC of intimidating them, but in the end the fare increase was removed.

**SOURCE 7** Albert Lutuli, President of the ANC, describes the Alexandra bus boycott of 1957

*66 Behind the headlines, what heroism there is! For the strong, a twenty-mile walk on top of a day's work is sufficient test of endurance. But what of the weak? What of the sick widow with five young children, whose only income comes from back-* *breaking labour? The weak walked too, setting out before there was a hint of sunrise and arriving home long after dark, exhausted. The patient endurance of the weak is stronger, far stronger, than the toughness of the bully with the gun. 99*

**SOURCE 8** People walking to work during the Alexandra bus boycott of 1957. The picture also gives a good idea of roads and houses in a black township

## Rural protests

One of the key policies of apartheid was to keep as many Africans as possible in rural areas. Under Verwoerd's apartheid (see pages 54–58) many Africans were forced to live in Bantustans, where, in theory at least, they ran their own affairs.

But the areas marked off for Africans to farm were too small, too poor, too over-stocked and too over-populated. When the government tried to organise a cattle-killing policy to improve the quality of the rest of the stock and to improve grazing grounds, there were widespread protests. The revolt in Pondoland went on for several years, although the government refused to give way and eventually stamped it out.

The chiefs were put in a difficult position. The government expected them to enforce white laws and to make their people carry passes and pay taxes. Some chiefs refused to co-operate and were removed. Others did co-operate, but were opposed by their people as 'puppets' of the apartheid government. These chiefs called in government police to crush the protests.

**SOURCE 9** Albert Lutuli describes the situation in rural South Africa

*66 Our home is the white man's garbage can. The land to which we have been relegated is aloes [a bitter-tasting plant] and stones. The people to whom land has been allocated are shabbily clad, their animals are feeble and bony. We have rural slums now. 99*

### ■ ACTIVITY

The only one of the protests described so far to succeed was the bus boycott. What lessons can you draw from this? Write a memo to the ANC leaders in 1959, suggesting what their future strategy should be. Include **four** action points.

# How did the government deal with resistance?

THE GOVERNMENT WAS determined to use all the forces it could to crush resistance. Its measures gradually became tougher and tougher, until by the 1980s black South Africans had hardly any civil rights at all. The Suppression of Communism Act (1950) meant that the South African Communist Party was banned and its members began to work inside other organisations, including the ANC. But the Act was also used to deal with anyone who opposed the regime. Belief in racial equality, for example, was regarded as 'Communist'. As Chapter 6 explains, this frantic opposition to 'the Communist menace' was one of the ways in which South Africa gained support from other Western countries during the Cold War.

## Banning orders

Under the Suppression of Communism Act anyone could be banned. There did not have to be a trial or proof, or even a charge. A person's freedom could be restricted in all sorts of ways, for years at a time, for no particular reason.

**SOURCE 1** Nelson Mandela describes being put under a banning order

*66 I found myself trailed by officers of the Security Branch wherever I went. In short, I found myself treated like a criminal – an unconvicted criminal. I was not allowed to pick my company, to join the company of others, participate in politics ... I was made, by the law, a criminal, not because of what I had done, but because of what I stood for, because of what I thought, because of my conscience. 99*

ANC leaders, as well as leaders of the Indian Congress and members of the Communist Party were put under banning orders. Often, a new banning order was made as soon as the previous one expired. Nelson Mandela was banned for most of the 1950s. So were most of the ANC leadership.

Activists like Nelson Mandela were:

forced to live in a certain place and prevented from leaving. Often they were kept in remote places, far from their homes and families

always being watched by the police

banned from meeting with others

banned from writing or broadcasting

banned from moving around the country freely.

# Mass arrests and the Treason Trial

The government did not hesitate to arrest large numbers of people. They did so after the Defiance Campaign, and in December 1956 they arrested 156 people connected with the Freedom Charter: 105 black Africans, 23 whites, 21 Indians and 7 Coloureds. Some of them had not even been at Kliptown on the day of the Charter Congress. They were accused of treason, of supporting Communism and belonging to a Communist organisation.

*The*
*ACCUSED*

*DECEMBER 1956*

**SOURCE 2** The 156 people arrested and tried for treason following the Freedom Charter Congress. This is actually a faked picture. The photographer had agreed with the police to take a photo of all 156 people on a sloping bank in the local park. Half an hour before the photo was due to be taken the police chief refused to allow it as the park was a 'whites only' park. So the photographer set up some benches and took several photographs, which he later mounted together

1. What difference would it have made if the photographer of Source 2 had issued the separate photos?
2. In what ways would you use this source, even though you know that it is faked?
3. This photo is often shown in books without saying that it is faked. Does this matter?

**SOURCE 3** Albert Lutuli describes his views on Communism

*66 I am in Congress because I am a Christian. The Communist philosophy I reject. But Communists are people and I will not regard them as less. I believe they are a misguided people. That makes me sorry for them. I do not find within myself a blind terror of the 'Communist menace'. 99*

The trial was badly organised and dragged on for years. While they were in jail together the accused were able to meet and plan. They were released on bail, so they could do their jobs but remained unable to carry out political activity. Eventually the government was unable to prove any of the charges. Most of the accused were obviously not Communists, and the evidence against those who were was unprovable. All were acquitted.

It was a kind of victory: the Freedom Charter and its demands for democracy got enormous publicity. However, the trial meant that many leaders were excluded from political activity for five long years.

## ■ TALKING POINTS

Some civil rights are to do with your rights at law. For example, your right to:

- be told what the charge is
- consult a lawyer of your choice
- be tried as soon as possible
- be given a fair trial.

1. Why are these rights important?
2. Which of these civil rights did not exist in South Africa under apartheid?

**SOURCE 4** Albert Lutuli describes being with the rest of the accused at the Treason Trial

*66 At last I could meet a really representative cross-section of my South Africa. The conditions of our lives in Johannesburg jail gave us the chance to meet men and women, famous and ordinary, and to find within us all a common loyalty and a common refusal to bow to government threats. The colour bar dropped away like the false and beastly thing it is. 99*

4. What surprising benefit did Albert Lutuli find from the mass arrests and the Treason Trial?

# W*hat happened at Sharpeville?*

**SOURCE 1**  A report of what happened at Sharpeville, 21 March 1960, from *Drum* magazine, a magazine for black readers

66 *Then the shooting started. We heard the chatter of a machine-gun, then another, then another. There were hundreds of women, some of them laughing. They must have thought the police were firing blanks. One woman was hit about ten yards from our car. Her companion, a young man, went back when she fell. He thought she had stumbled. He looked at the blood on his hands and said: 'My God, she's gone!'*

*Hundreds of children were running too.*

*Before the shooting I heard no warning to the crowd to disperse. There was no warning volley.*

*The police have claimed they were in desperate danger because the crowd was stoning them. The police have also said that the crowd was armed with 'ferocious weapons' which littered the area after they fled. I saw no weapons, although I looked carefully and afterwards studied the photographs of the death scene.* 99

THIS REPORT FROM *Drum* magazine describes one of the key events of South African history in the apartheid years. It was to be a turning-point for many individuals and for the country.

Who were these people at Sharpeville? Why were they there? And why did the police shoot at them? In this enquiry you will be looking at several sources about this key event and evaluating them in order to answer these questions.

## Background to Sharpeville: the creation of the Pan-African Congress

The way the ANC had developed in the 1950s – putting their efforts into the Freedom Charter and working with other races and groups – angered some black activists. Young blacks in the townships were disappointed at the ANC's lack of success. In 1959 Robert Sobukwe left the ANC and set up the Pan-African Congress (PAC) as a completely African resistance movement. Several years earlier, Anton Lembede (see page 66), a leader of the ANC Youth League had argued the case for a completely African resistance movement. Now 'Africanist' ideas were being heard from many parts of Africa, as black nationalists fought for their freedom from colonialism.

**SOURCE 2**  Robert Sobukwe, President and founder of the Pan-African Congress

**SOURCE 3**  Robert Sobukwe outlines the policy of the Pan-African Congress

66 *Government of the Africans by the Africans and for the Africans, with everybody who owes his only loyalty to Africa and is prepared to accept the democratic rule of the African majority being regarded as African.* 99

1.  How different does this quote suggest the PAC's policy was from that of the ANC?

Both the PAC and the ANC decided to campaign against the Pass Laws in 1959. The ANC announced single-day anti-pass marches; the PAC called for mass disobedience. The PAC decided to hold a mass civil disobedience demonstration at Sharpeville, about 20 km from Johannesburg, on 21 March 1960. They were going to refuse to carry passes and go to the police station demanding to be arrested.

The crowd arrived outside the police station. There was a minor scuffle and then suddenly the police opened fire. Sixty-nine people were killed and about 180 wounded. Meanwhile, at Langa, near Cape Town, police attacked another demonstration, killing 2 and wounding 49.

# ■ SOURCE INVESTIGATION

## What really happened at Sharpeville?

**S**OURCE 4  Sharpeville, 21 March 1960

**S**OURCE 5  Ambrose Reeves, Bishop of Johannesburg, describes events leading up to the shootings

*66 Gradually the news spread through the township that a statement concerning passes was to be made by some important person during the day at the police station and from about 8a.m. Africans started to gather round it. They waited patiently for the expected announcement and gradually the crowd grew.*

*Various estimates have been made of the crowd, and it would seem that, although there must have been a gathering of some thousands of Africans, press reports and the South African police almost certainly over-estimated the number. The Prime Minister read the official report on Sharpeville to the House of Assembly . . . In this report, the allegation was made that there were 20,000 people around the police station. Photographs show that it is unlikely that there were more than 5,000 people at any one time. 99*

**S**OURCE 6  An extract from a statement by the South African High Commissioner in London, 1960

*66 According to information now available, the disturbances at Sharpeville on Monday resulted from a planned demonstration of about 20,000 natives in which demonstrators attacked the police with assorted weapons, including firearms. The demonstrators shot first, and the police were forced to fire in self-defence and avoid even more tragic results. The allegation of the United Nations, that the demonstrators were unarmed and peaceful, is completely untrue. 99*

**S**OURCE 7  A description by Ambrose Reeves of discoveries made after the shootings

*66 The result of the firing was devastating and the figures which were established later, both at the post-mortem and at the hospital, show that over 70 per cent of the victims were clearly shot from the back. 99*

**S**OURCE 8  Sharpeville, later on the day of the shootings

1. What does Source 4 tell you about the situation before the shooting began?
2. To what extent do Sources 1 (see page 76) and 5 agree on what was happening?
3. Comment on the reliability of Sources 1 and 5 for finding out what really happened.
4. List the differences between the accounts given in Sources 1 and 5 and the account in Source 6.
5. Why do you think the South African government claimed that there were far more demonstrators than the other accounts said?
6. What reasons can you suggest for the other differences between the accounts?
7. What is the significance of the information in Source 7 about how people were shot?
8. How does Source 8 add to your understanding of what happened?
9. If you could have been there, what else would you like to have found out?
10. Write your own brief account, based on the sources here, of what you think happened on 21 March 1960 at Sharpeville.

# What were the results of Sharpeville?

**S**OURCE 1  The mass burial of people shot at Sharpeville

**S**OURCE 2  An extract from the speech given by Albert Lutuli as he accepted the Nobel Peace Prize in 1961

*66 Who will deny that thirty years of my life have been spent knocking in vain, patiently, moderately, and modestly at a closed and barred door. What have been the fruits of moderation? The past thirty years have seen the greatest number of laws restricting our rights, until today we have almost no rights at all. 99*

## ■ ACTIVITY

Historians have to be precise about events and dates.

1. Put the 12 cards below into the order in which you think the events took place.
a) What are your reasons for the order you have chosen?
b) Does this list fully explain the results of Sharpeville?

Historians also have to try to make sense of what was happening. This leads them to group events, to try to find patterns.

2. Try grouping the items in order of importance.
a) Which do you think are the three most and least important results on your list? Why?
b) Does this grouping help you to understand the significance of Sharpeville better?
3. Another pattern would be to look at the reactions to Sharpeville in different places: in the government; among the people of South Africa; from abroad.
    Sort the items under these three headings. What can you tell about government policy from its reactions to Sharpeville?

**1** Huge crowds attended the funerals of those killed.

**2** The government banned the ANC and the PAC.

**3** The ANC and the PAC abandoned non-violence and founded militant resistance organisations: the ANC setting up Umkhonto we Sizwe, usually abbreviated to MK (Spear of the Nation) and the PAC creating POQO (We alone).

**4** The ANC and PAC set up headquarters abroad. Oliver Tambo was given the job of winning international support for the ANC.

**5** Africans burnt pass books in protests all over South Africa.

**6** Africans held stay-at-home protests all over South Africa.

**7** The government arrested 18,000 people.

**8** The UN called for SANCTIONS against South Africa.

**9** Investors took their money out of South Africa. The government imposed currency restrictions.

**10** Young Africans left South Africa to train as guerrillas in China, the USSR and independent African countries.

**11** Anti-apartheid groups were set up in many countries, including Britain.

**12** The British Commonwealth Conference criticised South Africa; South Africa left the Commonwealth.

# What next for the ANC?

Sharpeville was the end of the line for non-violence as far as Nelson Mandela and many other members of the ANC were concerned. The police had killed 69 people; the government had made no statement of regret but instead had tried to justify what the police had done. The protests which followed were met with mass arrests. Then the ANC was banned.

What next?

Give up, go home to my wife Winnie, my child and my job as a lawyer?

Go abroad and persuade other countries to press for change in South Africa?

Continue with non-violence?

Begin an armed struggle?

Where can we get weapons from? The USSR would help, but will it matter if we get supplies from a Communist country?

Should we destroy offices, farms and houses belonging to whites? If we do this, innocent whites may be killed. Would it be better to destroy important places which do not involve any loss of life?

The ANC took up several of these options.

**a)** Albert Lutuli continued to practise non-violence.

**b)** Oliver Tambo left South Africa in 1960. The government banned him from returning and he travelled the world for the next 30 years, trying to persuade other governments to bring about change in South Africa. The ANC set up offices in Britain, Tanzania and elsewhere.

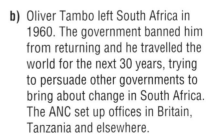

**c)** Nelson Mandela argued that the violence had already begun – started by the government. After much discussion within the ANC, they set up Umkhonto we Sizwe to carry out an armed struggle against apartheid.

**d)** White Communists in the ANC, such as Joe Slovo, used their connections with the USSR to get hold of weapons and explosives, although this led many Western countries to view the ANC with suspicion.

## The armed struggle begins

Umkhonto we Sizwe (usually known as MK) rejected all-out war against the white community, as it would involve killing innocent people. Instead, important but unstaffed targets, such as electricity pylons, were blown up. Later, deaths were caused by MK guerrillas.

**SOURCE 3** Damage to electricity pylons caused by a bomb planted by Umkhonto we Sizwe, December 1961

**SOURCE 4** An extract from a leaflet published by Umkhonto we Sizwe, December 1961

66 *We of Umkhonto have always sought to achieve liberation without bloodshed. We hope, even at this late hour, that our first actions will awaken everyone to a realisation of the disastrous situation to which the Nationalist policy is leading. We hope that we will bring the government and its supporters to their senses before it is too late, so that both the government and its policies can be changed before matters reach the desperate stage of* civil war ... *The time comes in the life of any nation when there remain only two choices: submit or fight. That time has now come to South Africa. We shall not submit and we have no choice but to hit back by all means within our power in defence of our people, our future and our freedom.*

*The government has interpreted the peacefulness of the movement as weakness; the people's non-violent policies have been taken as a green light for government violence ... We are striking out along a new road for the liberation of this country.* 99

Nelson Mandela went into hiding. He travelled around South Africa, organising MK. He used many disguises, claiming to be a chauffeur, or a gardener. Often he only just avoided the police. Sometimes he met Winnie in secret. In 1962 he travelled to several African countries and to Britain, talking to political leaders. But the BUREAU OF STATE SECURITY (BOSS) found out about his trip and arrested him on his return. The court sentenced him to five years in prison.

# The Rivonia Trial

MK continued its acts of sabotage and by mid-1963 some 200 had been carried out. Then the police found the MK base at Rivonia, a farm outside Johannesburg. Papers were found linking MK to acts of violence, and giving the names of organisers. Several were arrested and put on trial, along with Nelson Mandela (who was already in prison). They were charged with treason, which carried the death penalty. Mandela's four-hour opening speech rose above self-defence; it appealed to white South Africans to understand their black fellow-countrymen and -women and tried to deal with their fears about 'one person, one vote' democracy. It was to be 30 years before the ideas in this speech could be put into practice.

The eight defendants feared the worst: execution. Instead, they were sentenced to life imprisonment. They were sent at once to begin their sentences on Robben Island, an island prison off Cape Town.

**S**OURCE 5  An extract from the four-hour opening speech by Nelson Mandela at his trial in 1964

66 *The lack of human dignity experienced by Africans is the direct result of the policy of white supremacy. White supremacy implies black inferiority. Whites tend to regard Africans as a separate breed. They do not look upon them as people, with families of their own; they do not realise that they have emotions – that they fall in love like white people do; that they want to be with their wives and children, like white people want to be with theirs; that they want to earn enough money to support their families properly, to feed and clothe them and send them to school . . .*

*Africans want to be paid a living wage. Africans want to perform work which they are capable of doing, and not work which the government declares them capable of. Africans want to live where they obtain work, and not be chased out of an area because they were not born there. Africans want to own land in places where they work and not be obliged to live in rented houses which they can never call their own. We want to be part of the general population, and not be confined to living in ghettos. African men want to have their wives and children to live with them where they work, and not be forced into an unnatural existence in men's hostels. African women want to be with their menfolk and not be left permanently widowed in the reserves. We want to travel in our own country and seek work where we want to and not where the labour bureau tells us. We want a just share in the whole of South Africa; we want security and a stake in society.*

*Above all, we want equal political rights, because without them our disabilities will be permanent. I know this sounds revolutionary to the whites in this country, because the majority of voters will be Africans.*

*This makes the white man fear democracy. But this fear cannot be allowed to stand in the way of the only solution which will guarantee racial harmony and freedom for all. It is not true that enfranchisement of all will result in racial domination. Political division based on colour is entirely artificial and when it disappears, so will the domination of one colour group by another. The ANC has spent half a century fighting against racialism. When it triumphs it will not change that policy. This then is what the ANC is fighting for. Their struggle is a truly national one. It is a struggle of the African people, inspired by their own suffering and their own experience. It is a struggle to live.*

*During my lifetime I have dedicated myself to this struggle. I have fought against white domination and I have fought against black domination. I have cherished the ideal of a democratic and free society in which all persons live together in harmony and with equal opportunities. It is an ideal which I hope to live and achieve. But, if needs be, it is an ideal for which I am prepared to die.* 99

**S**OURCE 6 The eight defendants in the Rivonia Trial, including Nelson Mandela (top left) and Walter Sisulu (on Mandela's right)

## ■ TASK 1

1. Look at the long extract from Nelson Mandela's speech at his trial in 1964 (Source 5). He had been working for equal rights for nearly twenty years. He had seen the position of black South Africans become worse, not better. Now he was on trial for his life; he could expect the death sentence.
a) How do you think you might feel in his situation? Angry? Afraid? Sad? Bitter? What kind of speech would you make?
b) On the evidence of this extract, what is Mandela's mood?
2. How does this speech try to appeal to:
a) his judges?
b) white South Africans who might read it in their newspapers?
c) black South Africans?

## ■ TASK 2

Analyse the extract from Mandela's speech in Source 5. Your teacher will give you a copy.

1. Underline in **red** all sentences which explain that black Africans are normal human beings.
2. Underline in **blue** the points where Mandela explains that black Africans cannot live like normal human beings under apartheid.
3. Underline in **green** the places where he outlines his political demands.
4. Underline in **black** the points where he tries to calm the fears of whites.

This was the last public speech Nelson Mandela made for 26 years. Was it a threat? A warning? A plea for understanding? Describe in your own words what his 'message' was.

## ■ TALKING POINT

On page 76 Sharpeville was described as a 'turning-point'. Do you agree? In what ways did that event change the nature of resistance to apartheid? Was the resistance movement stronger or weaker as a result?

# How did Black Consciousness change people's lives?

IN THE 1960s black resistance to apartheid was at a low ebb. The ANC and the PAC were smashed, their leaders in exile or suffering long sentences in prison. Detention without trial was introduced in 1963: this meant that you could be arrested and held in prison for up to 90 days without being charged with any offence or having the opportunity to defend yourself in court. In the same year, for the first time a black prisoner died in police detention; his death was followed by many others. In 1965 the period of detention without trial was doubled to 180 days. Under Prime Minister John Vorster police powers were increased. The Bureau of State Security (BOSS) was almost above the law. The government was obviously prepared to use brute force and tough laws to crush all opposition.

But human beings cannot be crushed for ever. There are many ways in which skill and talent can show themselves and so prove that one person is as good as another (or better), whatever their skin colour. In South Africa blacks were banned from competing on equal terms in sport, so it was in the arts – music above all – that new talents emerged.

## Black South African music and literature

Some of the most talented black South African musicians had come to Britain in 1961 with the musical *King Kong*: Miriam Makeba, Todd Matshikiza, the Manhattan Brothers, Hugh Masekela and several others. None of them went back. However, many talented musicians remained in South Africa. Dollar Brand (Abdullah Ibrahim), Kippie Moeketsi and Mankuku Ngozi were all jazz musicians interested in combining African music with American jazz. *Shebeens* (see page 61) and clubs in black townships provided places for black musicians to play black music to black audiences. The Soweto Jazz Festival gave opportunities for black South African musicians to learn from each other.

Some jazz musicians were also poets; concerts often combined poetry readings with music. Black poets, like Denis Brutus, Oswald Mbuyiseni Mtshali and Mongane Wally Serote, wrote for black readers and had a large following. Black magazines, like *Drum*, carried their work to wide audiences. Later, radical white-run publishers, like Ravan Press, gave opportunities to black novelists and playwrights.

1. Why was black music so important to black South Africans?
2. Many black South African musicians went to live abroad as soon as they got a chance. Do you blame them for that? Explain your answer.

SOURCE 1 Hugh Masekela, playing in the St Peter's Huddleston Band, 1955

SOURCE 2 A poem written on Robben Island by Denis Brutus, a black poet

❝ *It is not all terror*
*And deprivation,*
*You know;*

*one comes to welcome the closer contact*
*and understanding one achieves*
*with one's fellow-men,*
*fellows, compeers;*

*and the discipline does much to force*
*a shape and pattern on one's daily life*
*as well as on the days*

*and honest toil*
*offers some redeeming hours*
*for the wasted years;*

*so there are times*
*when the mind is bright and restful*
*though alive;*
*rather like the full calm morning sea* ❞

# The Steve Biko story

## ■ TASK

Steve Biko was an interesting character. As you go through this section, try to imagine meeting him.

1. Note down:
   a) three things about his personality
   b) three things about his views on Black Consciousness
   c) three things he was good at in the Black Consciousness movement.
2. Why did the South African government regard this young student as such a threat to apartheid? Write your answer: 'Biko was regarded by the government as a threat to apartheid because he . . .'

**1.** Steve Biko was born in 1946. His father died when he was four and his mother struggled to bring up the family and to give her children an education.

**2.** Universities were segregated. At the medical school of Natal University, Biko found himself among some of the cleverest black students in South Africa. Biko soon emerged as the clearest, most exciting thinker about Black Consciousness.

> If we think of ourselves as inferior to whites, apartheid will have won!

> Apartheid calls us 'non-whites' – just by calling ourselves black, we strike a blow against the government!

**6.** Biko and his friends read the writings of Martin Luther King and Malcolm X, black activists campaigning for civil rights in the USA.

**7.** In 1969 Biko set up a students' union for blacks only – the South African Students' Organisation (SASO). He wrote a column in the student newspaper under the name 'Frank Talk'.

## I WRITE WHAT I LIKE

BY FRANK TALK

The black man has become a shell, a shadow of a man, completely defeated, drowning in his own misery, a slave. No wonder the African child learns to hate his heritage in his days at school. So negative is the image presented to him that he finds comfort only in close identification with white society. Part of the approach in bringing about Black Consciousness has to be directed to the past, to seek to rewrite the history of the black man and to produce in it the heroes who form the core of the African background.

**10.** He helped to set up a health centre called Zanenphilo (which means 'The one bringing health'), run by Dr Ramphele, his lover.

> I've got to go back home to King Williams Town but I'm not going to let the whites stop me working.

**11.** The Black People's Convention also helped to set up Njwaxa, a cottage industry in which unemployed blacks produced leather goods.

> This centre will be run by blacks, for blacks!

**3. Black Consciousness was about . . .**

- pride in being black
- refusing to accept white superiority
- refusing to accept help, even from friendly whites – blacks could achieve by themselves
- knowing about black African heroes of the past.

**4.** Biko described watching a pair of workmen installing electricity in a house . . .

The white boss was abusing the black man the whole time, calling him foul names. I asked the black man why he put up with it. At first, he said it didn't bother him, he was used to it . . .

**5.**

But once we were on our own he told me how he really felt . . .

It makes me mad to have to stand there and take it, but what can I do? I need the job.

**8.** Biko travelled all over South Africa. He became known as a powerful speaker and someone who never let the white authorities treat him with disrespect.

It didn't matter where in South Africa, in rural areas or in townships, in towns or the suburbs, we always knew where to go, which shebeen to go to. We would arrive in a place, sometimes at three in the morning. We would knock, the person would say no, but as soon as they heard it was us they would open and we would get six boxes of beer and two quarts of whisky and a gumba [a party] started . . . We would all be tired and I would fall asleep and wake up and Steve would still be in his chair, talking and drinking. And the thing that struck you was his great joy at being among people.

Wally Serote, a friend of Steve Biko in his student days, describes what it was like to hang out with him

**9.** In 1972 he was thrown out of Natal University for neglecting his studies. Biko began to work for the Black Consciousness Convention, which set up self-help projects for poor black people, but he was banned in 1973.

**12.** In 1976 the school pupils of Soweto started an uprising which spread to other townships. Biko had had no contact with the pupils but the students were inspired by Biko's ideas,

Steve Biko is a dangerous man! Arrest him!

**13.** Biko was arrested in September 1977. He was kept naked in a cell for eighteen days, beaten up and chained to a grille. He was then tipped into the back of a Land Rover, and driven 1,600 km to hospital, where he died. He was 30 years old . . .

## The death of Steve Biko

Steve Biko was the forty-fifth person to die in police custody since the introduction of detention without trial in 1963. There was international disgust, not only at his death but at the police cover-up which followed it. The truth about what happened to him did not emerge until twenty years later, in the hearings of the TRUTH AND RECONCILIATION COMMISSION (see page 136).

> **S**OURCE 3  The government explanation of what happened to Steve Biko, reported in the *Cape Times*, 14 September 1977
>
> 66 *The political leader Mr Stephen Biko died while in security police custody, eight days after he began a hunger strike, the Minister of Justice, Mr Jimmy Kruger, said yesterday.*
> *Mr Kruger detailed how Mr Biko, 30, refused meals and water from September 5ᵗʰ, and how he was examined by various doctors, then sent to a prison hospital in Port Elizabeth, taken back to police cells and finally transferred to Pretoria where he died on the night of his arrival.* 99

3. What does Source 3 tell you about the attitudes of the South African government at that time?

> **S**OURCE 4  A report from the CNN website of the hearings of the Truth and Reconciliation Commission, 1997
>
> 66 *January 28 SOUTH AFRICAN OFFICERS CONFESS TO KILLING BIKO. Former South African security officers have confessed to killing anti-apartheid activist Steve Biko, according to a statement released by the country's Truth and Reconciliation Commission.*
> *September 10 Major Harold Snyman is among five white former policemen implicated in the death of Biko ... but while Snyman testified he took part in a brutal interrogation and cover-up, he claimed Biko's death was an accident ... Snyman, 69, testified that Biko spent at least a day in an apparently unconscious state, shackled to a grille with his legs and arms outspread.* 99

4. How do you think Steve Biko changed black people's attitude to their situation?
5. What effect do you think this had on black resistance to apartheid?

### ■ ACTIVITY

Look back at the families described on pages 59–61. How do you think the members of each family would react to the death of Steve Biko? Choose one of the families and script a conversation between the family members.

### ■ TALKING POINT

Biko's wife, Ntsiki, does not think it is right that Major Snyman and the four other policemen who were involved in Biko's death should go free after confessing their guilt to the Truth and Reconciliation Commission. What do you think?

**S**OURCE 5  A poster carried at the funeral of Steve Biko, 1977

> **S**OURCE 6  A description of Steve Biko by Lindy Wilson in *Bounds of Possibility*, a book published in 1991
>
> 66 *It is not his death, but his life – Steve Biko's life-giving force – which concerns us. Biko had a vitality which drew people to him, not only for his advice, but for his exuberance, not only for his extraordinary clear thinking, but his love of life, his capacity to listen, his capacity to learn. His gift of leadership was not of the kind that people followed him in a slavish kind of way, but that suddenly, and to their great surprise, they got to know themselves.* 99

# What were the results of the black workers' strikes of 1973?

THERE IS A long history of trade union action among both blacks and whites in South Africa. The government clampdown of the 1960s crushed all black trade union activity and there were almost no strikes. It was also a time of rising wages for black workers.

In 1973 there was a worldwide economic crisis. South African workers suffered wage reductions, longer hours and poorer working conditions. These changes led to a series of serious strikes in Natal: 200,000 workers were involved.

The important thing for a strike to succeed is solidarity: workers all acting together can force their employer to make changes; as individuals, they cannot. Trade union organisation was still weak but the Natal workers were mostly Zulus, commuting to work from the Zulu homeland. They were encouraged by their Zulu leaders. They were united by their ethnic loyalty, and traditional Zulu weapons appeared at strike meetings. The employers were forced to give way and restore wages to their previous levels.

Many workers learned the lesson of 1973; and trade union activity revived again. Trade unions were to play a big part in the eventual collapse of apartheid.

1. Trade union organisation was not strong in 1973. What clue is there in Source 1 about another type of organisation to which workers in Natal belonged, which had the same effect as a trade union?
2. What does Source 2 tell you about the reaction of the South African government to the strikes?

**SOURCE 1** Zulu workers waving weapons at a trade union meeting in Natal, 1973

**SOURCE 2** Police at a strike meeting in Durban, 1973

# Why did the school students of Soweto riot in 1976?

**SOURCE 1** **SOURCE 1** This picture flashed across the world on the evening of 16 June 1976. It changed many people's minds about apartheid. It shows Hector Peterson, a thirteen-year-old boy, being rushed away by his grief-stricken friends after being shot dead by South African police in Soweto. Why was a young boy shot by police? What was it all about?

## Life in the townships

The burden of apartheid still weighed as heavily as ever in the black townships in 1976. The economy was not doing so well, and many people were unemployed. House-building in Soweto had slowed down and there was terrible overcrowding.

The Bantustans were about to become independent (see pages 54–57). People in the townships were afraid that they would be forced to live in the Bantustans in even greater poverty.

A new local government system was being set up. This kept power in the hands of the white government, with the help of a few blacks who were willing to work with them, but it made black residents pay for local services such as roads and schools.

## Conditions in schools

The original plan for apartheid had been for black children to be given only primary education, as this was all they would need for the manual jobs they would always do. But by the 1970s South African business and industry needed better educated people to work in their offices and factories. Black children wanted to be educated: the numbers of black children in schools rose from 1 million in 1950 to 3.5 million in 1975. Only 8 per cent of these were in secondary education, but the demand was rising

fast. Yet the quality of education available was terrible, reflecting the fact that the government spent nearly ten times more on educating each white child than on each black child. Schools were run down. In Soweto, there were often 60 or even 100 children in a class. Teachers were badly trained and poorly paid. The result of all this was that black children's tremendous hopes and expectations for education were frustrated.

Added to all this were two other factors.

- Black Consciousness had had an impact on many students, even though Steve Biko had not made any attempt to work with people of their age.
- In 1975 the white Portuguese colonial rulers of Mozambique and Angola had been thrown out by black independence movements, despite the support the South African government had given them.

Then the government announced that half of all the subjects students took in schools, including Maths, Geography and History, would be taught in Afrikaans. This was the last straw. Afrikaans was the language of the hated government. It was spoken only by South African whites, and not even by all of them. It had no value to students wanting to travel. It was only suitable for jobs that involved taking orders from Afrikaners.

# Demonstrations

On 16 June 1976, 15,000 students held a demonstration in part of Soweto. The police fired at them and two students were killed. One of them was Hector Peterson (see Source 1). There was an outcry. More demonstrations were held, in Soweto and other parts of South Africa. The police used more violence and more students were killed. Students boycotted classes and burnt schools. They attacked *shebeens*, saying that brew-houses were taking money from their fathers' pockets which should have gone on their families. Government forces encouraged migrant workers (from outside South Africa and from other areas of the country) to beat up demonstrators. At the end of the year, the government said that 600 people had been killed: the true figure was probably 1,000.

Hector Peterson (see Source 1)

## ■ ACTIVITY

1. Write daily diary entries for a schoolboy or schoolgirl in Soweto for the week of 16 June 1976. Describe:
   a) what you have done
   b) why you have done these things
   c) how you feel about them.
2. Now write a short press statement from the South African government, saying what has happened, as you see it, and telling the world why.

**S**OURCE 2  Steve Biko describes the young people of the Soweto riots

❝ *The dramatic thing about the bravery of those youths is that they have now discovered that the bond between life and death is absolute: you are either alive and proud. Or you are dead, and when you are dead you can't care anyway. And your method of death can be a political act, so you die in the riots. For a hell of a lot of them there's nothing to lose, so if you overcome your fear of death, you're on your way.* ❞

**S**OURCE 3  Winnie Mandela describes what she saw in Soweto in 1976

❝ *I was there among them, I saw what happened. The children picked up stones, they used dustbin lids as shields and marched towards the machine-guns ... The determination, the thirst for freedom in children's hearts, was such that they were prepared to face those machine-guns with stones. That is what happens when you hunger for freedom, when you want to break those chains of oppression, nothing else seems to matter.* ❞

**S**OURCE 4  Students demonstrating in Soweto in 1976. Shortly after this picture was taken South African police fired into the crowd to disperse the rioters, and witnesses claim three people were killed

## What were the results of the Soweto schools' protests?

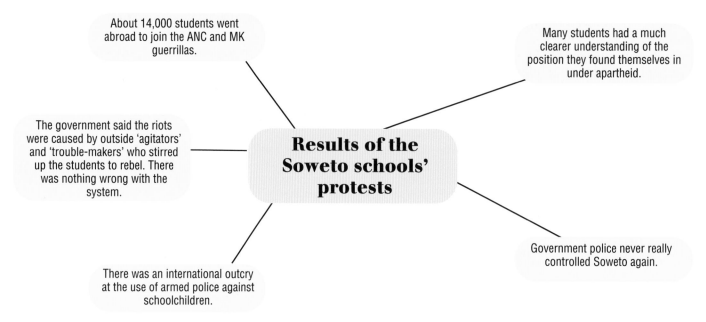

About 14,000 students went abroad to join the ANC and MK guerrillas.

Many students had a much clearer understanding of the position they found themselves in under apartheid.

The government said the riots were caused by outside 'agitators' and 'trouble-makers' who stirred up the students to rebel. There was nothing wrong with the system.

**Results of the Soweto schools' protests**

Government police never really controlled Soweto again.

There was an international outcry at the use of armed police against schoolchildren.

**SOURCE 5** An extract from *A Different Kind of War* by Julie Frederickse (Ravan Press, 1986) in which three students in Soweto talk about their reactions to the 1976 protests

❝ *Siphiwe:* '*The thing that made me politically minded was the influence I got from 1976 because so many of our brothers and sisters were shot dead for their rights. In fact, 16 June 1976 was the day I started to have an interest in political activity in this country.*'
*Ben:* '*My awareness was limited because of my education, the things we were told at school. One of the things they wanted us to believe was that nobody can change the system, that it is God's will. But because of the challenge that was presented to the system by the students, I began to realise that, no, these things are manmade and it is possible to change the system.*'
*Jabulani:* '*It was the 1976 experience that made us ask questions, you know, about the poverty of our people, the living conditions of our people. We started questioning why whites live that type of life and we live in these conditions. We began to realise also that the whole education system is a very big lie.*' ❞

### ■ TASK

List the causes of the Soweto schools' protests of 1976. Once you have a simple list, make it into a spider diagram.

1. Put the word PROTEST in the middle of the page. Write the immediate (or 'trigger') causes near it.
2. Add more long-lasting or more distant causes further away.
3. Then draw lines to show links between causes: write the link on the line.

### ■ TALKING POINT

Look at the diagram showing the results of the Soweto protests. Some people called the protests 'The beginning of the end of apartheid'. Explain how each of the results could suggest that apartheid must end one day.

# Conclusion: How did black resistance to apartheid change between 1948 and 1976?

## ■ TASK 1

1. Look again at the timeline in Source 6 on page 65. On your own copy:
   a) underline in **red** all the anti-apartheid protest and resistance actions where the aims of the action were **political**, that is, concerned with votes, or personal freedom, or civil rights
   b) underline in **blue** all those where the aims of the action were **economic**, that is, concerned with jobs, trying to make ends meet, money
   c) underline in **green** all those where the aims of the action were **cultural**, that is, about attitudes.

   In some cases you may need to use more than one colour for an action.

2. What patterns can you see in the anti-apartheid resistance of these years?

## ■ TASK 2

1. After 28 years of protest apartheid was as firmly rooted in South Africa as ever and the lives of black people were as bad as ever, if not worse. Some people have said that the reasons for this failure of resistance to achieve anything much are that:
   a) resistance leaders **over-estimated** the willingness of the people to rise up in great numbers
   b) they **under-estimated** the readiness of the government to use force to crush resistance.

   Do you agree with either or both of these statements? Use the information from this chapter to support your conclusion.

2. Look at the resistance actions described on pages 87–90. They are said to mark the beginning of the end of apartheid. What is there in each of them which could bring apartheid to an end?

**SOURCE 1** High school students erect barricades on the streets of Soweto

# Postscript: What happened to Nelson Mandela between 1964 and 1989?

FOLLOWING THE LIFE sentence he received at the Rivonia Trial in 1964, Nelson Mandela was sent to the prison for black political prisoners on Robben Island. He was aged almost 46. He was to stay on Robben Island for eighteen years, as Prisoner 466/64, until he was moved to a prison on the mainland for another eight years.

Robben Island is a small, rocky island 11 km out in Cape Town Bay. The Dutch had used it as early as 1658 to imprison a Khoi chief, Autshumayo. Later, the British had used it to get chiefs opposed to their conquest of southern Africa out of the way: Chief Makana was held there in 1819 and Chief Maqoma in 1850. Both these men were Xhosas, like Mandela. Mandela drew strength from the knowledge that other black leaders in the struggle against white rule had been held in the prison before him.

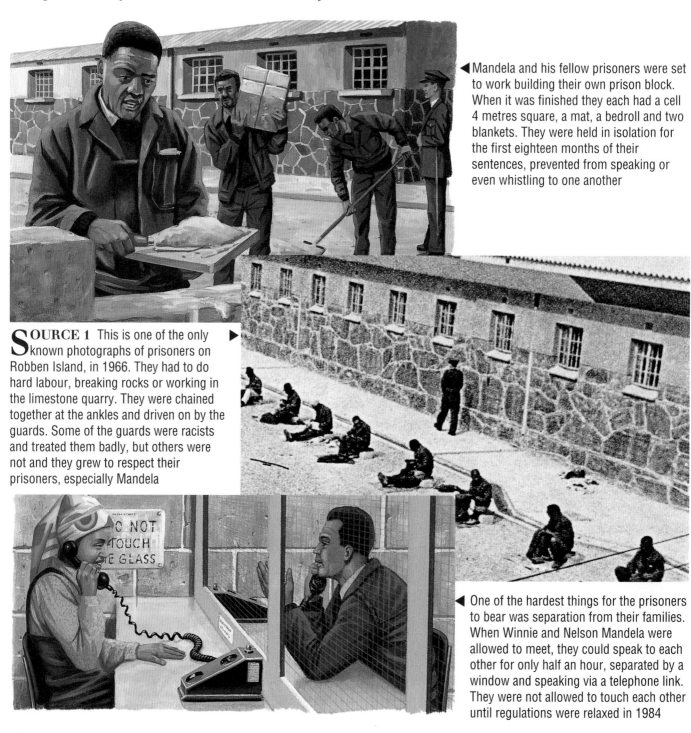

◀ Mandela and his fellow prisoners were set to work building their own prison block. When it was finished they each had a cell 4 metres square, a mat, a bedroll and two blankets. They were held in isolation for the first eighteen months of their sentences, prevented from speaking or even whistling to one another

**SOURCE 1** This is one of the only known photographs of prisoners on Robben Island, in 1966. They had to do hard labour, breaking rocks or working in the limestone quarry. They were chained together at the ankles and driven on by the guards. Some of the guards were racists and treated them badly, but others were not and they grew to respect their prisoners, especially Mandela

◀ One of the hardest things for the prisoners to bear was separation from their families. When Winnie and Nelson Mandela were allowed to meet, they could speak to each other for only half an hour, separated by a window and speaking via a telephone link. They were not allowed to touch each other until regulations were relaxed in 1984

# Winnie Mandela

Nelson Mandela had married Winnie, who was younger than him, in 1958 and at the time of the Rivonia Trial they had daughters aged four and six. Winnie was already active in politics before their marriage. After Nelson was imprisoned she became the focus of international – and government – attention. She had long banning orders imposed on her and was placed under house arrest. She was forced to move from her Soweto home to a tiny, remote town called Brandfort. In order to visit her husband, she had to make a journey of 1,600 km, then take the ferry out to the island. She was not allowed to take their children with her. Winnie paid a high price for Nelson's imprisonment and they both worked to keep the relationship going.

**SOURCE 2** Winnie describes feeling guilty about not being able to be a normal mother because of banning orders

*66 I was never there as a mother to hold my little girls' hands, take them to school and introduce them to their teachers, as is the glory of every mother when her children start school. I've never entered any of the schools attended by my children. I've never met any of my children's teachers. 99*

Mandela tried to come to terms with his long imprisonment. He worked hard at keeping fit, waking at 3.30a.m. each day to do two hours' exercise before work. In the evenings he studied law. He became the leader of the little group of prisoners, arguing calmly but firmly for their basic rights as prisoners. Together, they educated themselves in politics, history and literature. For example, they read Shakespeare in the evenings, then discussed his ideas about leadership during their work in the quarry the following day. In this way Mandela kept himself mentally and physically strong.

**SOURCE 4** The prisoners had to support each other emotionally, too. Nelson Mandela later recalled how Walter Sisulu supported him when Mandela heard that his only son by his first marriage had been killed in a car crash in 1969

*66 I do not have words to express the sorrow or loss I felt. I returned to my cell and lay on my bed. Finally Walter came to me and knelt beside my bed and I handed him the telegram. He said nothing, but only held my hand. I do not know how long he remained with me. 99*

The world did not forget Nelson Mandela. Through the work of the ANC, Winnie Mandela and, later, their two daughters, his name was often in the news. When apartheid began to go badly wrong for the government in the 1980s, the 'Free Nelson Mandela' campaign gained new momentum.

## ■ ACTIVITY

You are one of the Rivonia Trial prisoners on Robben Island. You have received a letter from someone in Amnesty International, asking how you are coping with your conditions and your sentence. Write a reply. What are the worst things about your situation?

**SOURCE 3** Nelson Mandela and Walter Sisulu on Robben Island in 1966

# WHY DIDN'T THE REST OF THE WORLD STOP APARTHEID?

## *Why did belief in white supremacy change?*

FOR MOST OF its existence, apartheid was widely criticised by people all over the world. This really annoyed the supporters of apartheid. They said, quite rightly, that their belief in white rule was little different from the system in many white-run colonies before the Second World War. The belief that white people were superior to black people was widespread in Europe right up until the mid-twentieth century.

> **SOURCE 1** The British writer John Ruskin, speaking at Oxford University in the 1870s
>
> 66 *We are a race mingled of the best northern blood ... This is what England must do or perish: she must found colonies as fast and as far as she is able ... seizing every piece of fruitful waste ground she can set her foot on.* 99

> **SOURCE 2** A magistrate in the Dutch colony at the Cape said in 1803
>
> 66 *A heathen is not actually human. His word cannot be believed and only by violent means can he do good and shun evil.* 99

But as the Second World War came to an end, world opinion was changing. The crucial turning-point was the Holocaust. Hitler began treating Jews as less than full citizens of Germany from 1933. The so-called 'Final Solution', his plan to exterminate all the Jews in Europe, began in 1941. Allied governments knew about it, but it was not until Allied troops invaded Germany and Poland in 1944 that reporters and photographers told the world what had been happening. Using 'superior' European technology, the Nazis had put to death six million Jews, four million Russians and up to a million others.

News of the Holocaust put paid to any idea of European racial superiority. The years just after the war saw major shifts in attitude. The United Nations included declarations of racial equality in its charter, signed in 1945. The Universal Declaration of Human Rights was agreed by the UN in 1948, the very year apartheid began. Non-white people all over the world began to claim their rights. This was one of the reasons why European empires began to crumble rapidly. India, the 'jewel in the crown' of the British Empire, became independent in 1947. By the mid-1970s there were only a few white-ruled colonies left in Africa or anywhere else in the world.

But South Africa did not follow this changing mood. Indeed it moved in the opposite direction. By the late 1970s, apartheid had been in existence for 30 years. It was successful and seemingly secure. Although out of step with almost every other country in the world, South Africa seemed to be getting away with it. In this chapter we will look at what the rest of the world might have done about apartheid, and why it failed.

**SOURCE 3** Concentration camp victims put to death by the Nazis, discovered by American soldiers who had just entered the camp, 1945

### ■ TALKING POINTS

How do you make people obey rules if they don't want to? Here are some examples to help you think about the issues.

1. Pupil A is bullying younger children at your school. What choices have **you** got in deciding how to deal with this person?
2. You know that Mr B, living in another part of Britain, is breeding cats in terrible, overcrowded conditions. What choices of action have **you** got? Should you act on your own? Work with others? Call in the police?
3. The government of Country C is torturing children. What choices have **you** got? Should you leave it to the British government to deal with? How can you make the government deal with another government which is behaving badly?

# How did the rest of the world try to bring about change in South Africa?

## ■ TASK

We are going to look at the different ways in which people and governments tried to persuade or force the South African government to abandon apartheid:

■ armed force   ■ sanctions
■ actions by ordinary people.

They all failed – or at least they were failing up to the late 1970s. As you work through this section, use a copy of the table opposite to note down the reasons why each method of persuading the South African government to change its ways failed.

| | Actions by South African government | Attitudes of other countries | Actions of other countries | Chance/accident |
|---|---|---|---|---|
| Armed force | | | | |
| Sanctions | | | | |
| Actions by ordinary people | | | | |

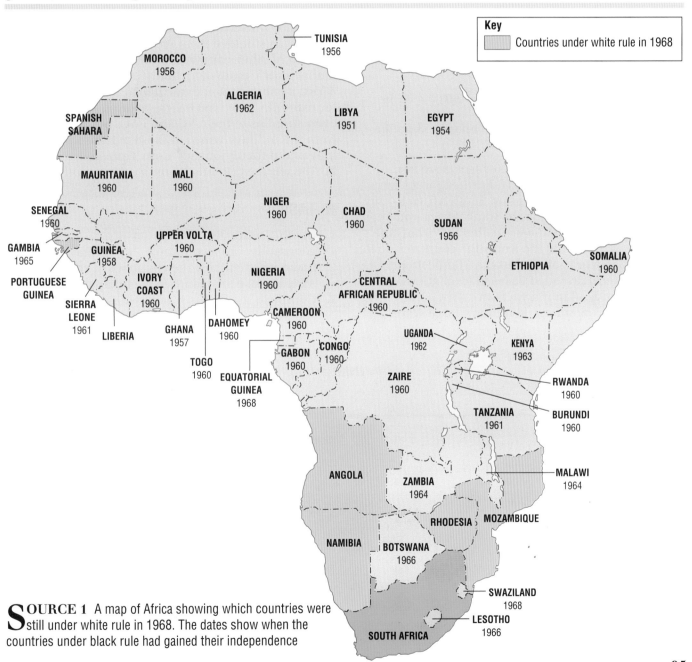

**SOURCE 1** A map of Africa showing which countries were still under white rule in 1968. The dates show when the countries under black rule had gained their independence

**Key**
Countries under white rule in 1968

TUNISIA 1956
MOROCCO 1956
ALGERIA 1962
LIBYA 1951
EGYPT 1954
SPANISH SAHARA
MAURITANIA 1960
MALI 1960
NIGER 1960
CHAD 1960
SUDAN 1956
SENEGAL 1960
GAMBIA 1965
PORTUGUESE GUINEA
GUINEA 1958
UPPER VOLTA 1960
NIGERIA 1960
CENTRAL AFRICAN REPUBLIC 1960
ETHIOPIA
SOMALIA 1960
SIERRA LEONE 1961
LIBERIA
IVORY COAST 1960
GHANA 1957
DAHOMEY 1960
TOGO 1960
CAMEROON 1960
GABON 1960
CONGO 1960
EQUATORIAL GUINEA 1968
ZAIRE 1960
UGANDA 1962
KENYA 1963
RWANDA 1960
TANZANIA 1961
BURUNDI 1960
ANGOLA
ZAMBIA 1964
MALAWI 1964
RHODESIA
MOZAMBIQUE
NAMIBIA
BOTSWANA 1966
SWAZILAND 1968
LESOTHO 1966
SOUTH AFRICA

# 1. Armed force

When apartheid began in 1948, almost all of Africa was ruled by the white colonial powers. Twenty years later, the situation was quite different (see Source 1). Only a handful of countries were not ruled by black Africans. In 1963 the newly independent nations of Africa formed the Organisation of African Unity (OAU). One of the first priorities of the OAU was to end apartheid. In 1969 several African nations met at Lusaka, in Zambia, to issue the Lusaka Manifesto (see Source 2).

1. Many whites living in the British, French and Belgian colonies in Africa returned to their European homelands when independence came. As we saw in Chapter 1, Afrikaners had lost contact with their European homeland, Holland, in the eighteenth century. How might this fact make the situation in South Africa different from other African countries?
2. How does the first sentence of Source 2 try to reassure white South Africans?
3. Why would the supporters of apartheid not be reassured by this offer?

For reasons you will see later (see page 98), Western nations with powerful armed forces were not prepared to declare war on South Africa to end apartheid. Countries close to South Africa and keen to overthrow apartheid were called the 'front-line' countries. What could the front-line countries do to turn the fine words of the Lusaka Manifesto into action? Several provided bases to train guerrilla fighters from Umkhonto we Sizwe (MK). But geography, economics and military force were against them.

**S**OURCE 2  Extracts from the Lusaka Manifesto of 1969

*66 We believe that all the peoples who have made their homes in southern Africa are Africans, regardless of the colour of their skins.*

*We have always preferred, and still prefer, to achieve liberation without physical violence. But while peaceful progress is blocked by those at present in power, we have no choice but to give to the peoples of those territories all the support of which we are capable in their struggle against their oppressors. 99*

As you can see on the map in Source 3, South Africa was shielded from its enemies to the north by a group of other countries under white rule. These 'buffer states' made it virtually impossible for South Africa's enemies to the north to attack it. Tanzania, for example, provided bases, training facilities and even supplies to the ANC and PAC. But guerrillas from the military wings of these organisations had a long and difficult journey from Tanzania, across hostile territory, to reach South African soil.

## ■ TASK

1. In what ways did:
a) geography   b) economics   c) military force make it difficult for the countries of southern Africa to use armed force to end apartheid?
2. Complete the first row of the table on page 95, showing how armed force affected the situation.

---

Angola and **Mozambique** were Portuguese colonies; Portugal was the only European country still clinging on to its colonies.

**South-West Africa** (also called Namibia) had been taken from Germany under the terms of the Treaty of Versailles at the end of the First World War, and given to South Africa.

**Rhodesia** (now Zimbabwe) was a British colony with about 240,000 white settlers and 4 million black Africans. Britain wanted to give Rhodesia independence on the basis of 'one person, one vote'. White Rhodesians refused to accept this and declared their own independence under white rule in 1965. South Africa supported them against Britain and the United Nations. Soon a civil war began and South Africa sent military help to the whites.

Although **Botswana**, **Lesotho** and **Swaziland** were under black rule, they were poor and under-populated. Lesotho and Swaziland were also surrounded, or almost surrounded, by South African territory. They could not afford to upset their powerful neighbour.

**South Africa** was rich, so it could afford an army and air force that were well-trained, well-equipped and increasing in size; it had by far the strongest military forces in Africa.

Migrant workers from all the nations of southern and eastern Africa worked in South Africa's gold mines. Most of their trade was with South Africa too, and they used South African ports for their exports. It would have been economic suicide for them to go to war with South Africa.

Key
- Black rule
- White rule

**S**OURCE 3  The 'buffer states' protecting South Africa

# 2. Sanctions

**Sanctions** are punishments, designed to make people behave better. For example, sanctions at school might be detention or extra work. It is hard to impose sanctions on a country, but one way of doing it is to cut off all kinds of links between the country that is in the wrong and other nations. Cutting trade links is the toughest form of sanctions, but sanctions could include refusing to take part in sporting fixtures or educational links, or artists refusing to perform in the country. The point is that sanctions should affect the lives of ordinary people, who would then put pressure on their government to change.

## The United Nations

The process of DECOLONISATION which changed the map of Africa and the rest of the world created lots more new independent nations. By the 1970s membership of the United Nations had doubled since its formation, to over a hundred members, and non-white nations were in a majority. Not surprisingly, therefore, the United Nations was among the first to condemn apartheid – in 1952. This condemnation grew stronger over the years. In 1966 the United Nations tried to make South Africa hand back South-West Africa (Namibia), the MANDATE it had held since 1919. South Africa refused and merely absorbed the territory into its country. All-white elections were held in Namibia to the South African Parliament. A Namibian independence movement, SWAPO (South-West African People's Organisation), began a civil war, but strong South African forces were, for the time being, successful. The UN continued to criticise South Africa and in the end expelled it completely in 1974. But what else could the UN do?

In 1962 it proposed tough economic sanctions: cutting off all trade links with South Africa, particularly in essential supplies such as oil. This kind of 'economic war' was supposed to force the South African government to change, or face economic ruin.

However, in order to work, sanctions have to have 100 per cent support. If one or two countries break the trade ban it doesn't work at all. Sanctions also require more from some countries than from others: it was up to those with lots of trade with South Africa to make sanctions work. The countries trading most with South Africa in these years were Britain, USA, Germany and Japan. They did not want to impose tough sanctions on South Africa.

## Why did sanctions fail in the 1960s and 1970s?

1. **Investments.** Lots of British, German, American and Japanese people and companies had invested money in South Africa. The South African economy was doing very well, with growth of 5–7 per cent in the 1960s. Investors were making a lot of money. They did not want to pull out.

> **SOURCE 4** A British writer, Charles Lonford, explains the attraction of South African investments
>
> *❝ The apartheid system was carefully designed to remove all obstacles in the way of exploitation of black labour. South Africa became an investor's paradise. Foreign capitalists, especially from Britain and the USA, invested in South Africa at the rate of 150 million rand per year, eagerly taking advantage of the oppression of the black masses. ❞*

2. **Minerals.** South Africa not only had large supplies of diamonds and gold but also some of the rare minerals which modern industry cannot do without (see Source 6).

> **SOURCE 5** A business executive's explanation of the importance of South Africa's mineral reserves
>
> *❝ Without chromium, cobalt, manganese and the platinum group of metals you couldn't build a jet engine, or a car, run a train, build an oil refinery or a power station. You couldn't process food, or run a sanitary [hygienic] restaurant or hospital operating theatre. You couldn't build a computer. ❞*

The efforts South Africa made to keep up good relations with Western governments are shown by the 'Muldergate' scandal, which eventually brought down Prime Minister John Vorster in 1978. Mulder was Vorster's right-hand man, and was given 64 million rand (£40 million), in secret, to win friends and influence people abroad, particularly in Britain, the USA and Japan. He paid magazines to publish favourable articles about South Africa; he bought luxury flats where influential figures could be entertained; some money was simply used to bribe politicians to make pro-South Africa speeches, or block anti-apartheid actions. When news of this secret fund and the ways it was used came to light, Vorster had to resign.

**S**OURCE 6  John Vorster, Prime Minister of South Africa 1966–78

### The Cold War

Throughout the years from 1945 to 1989 the world was divided between the Eastern, Communist bloc of countries, led by the USSR, and the Western, CAPITALIST bloc of countries, led by the USA. The two sides became involved in a 'cold' war against each other, that is, a war waged in ways short of actually fighting each other. One of the ways the two sides confronted each other was over control of the world's resources, and Africa was one of the places where they struggled for influence.

South Africa was a strongly capitalist, pro-Western country during the Cold War. It was fiercely opposed to Communism. Western leaders feared what would happen if South Africa fell into Communist hands. Not only their investments, not only the minerals, but the strongest bastion of capitalism in Africa would be lost. They looked at the huge amounts of oil carried around the Cape from the Middle East to Europe and the USA. They imagined what a hold the USSR would have over them if South Africa's harbours were full of Soviet submarines. The South African government played up these fears for all they were worth. Ministers made speeches exaggerating the Soviet threat.

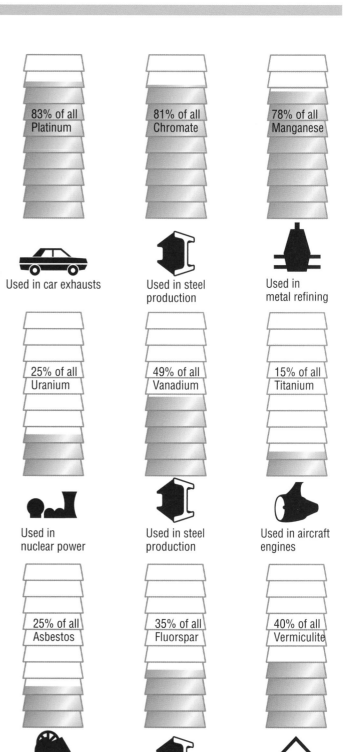

83% of all Platinum — Used in car exhausts

81% of all Chromate — Used in steel production

78% of all Manganese — Used in metal refining

25% of all Uranium — Used in nuclear power

49% of all Vanadium — Used in steel production

15% of all Titanium — Used in aircraft engines

25% of all Asbestos — Used in cement

35% of all Fluorspar — Used in steel production

40% of all Vermiculite — Used in insulation

**S**OURCE 7  The developed world depended on South Africa's mineral wealth. This diagram shows the percentage of total world supplies of vital minerals which South Africa held and their uses in industry

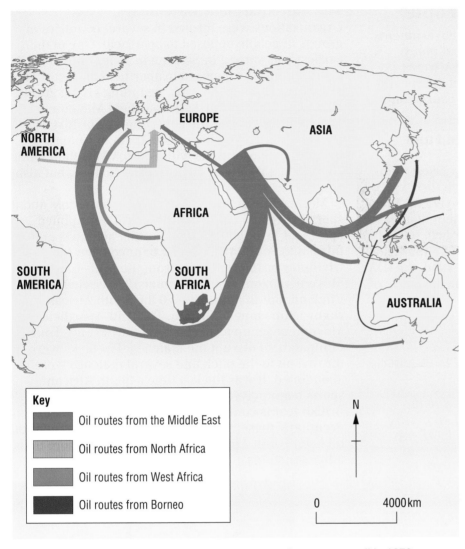

**Key**
- Oil routes from the Middle East
- Oil routes from North Africa
- Oil routes from West Africa
- Oil routes from Borneo

N

0        4000 km

S**OURCE 8** A map showing the major routes used to transport oil in 1973

S**OURCE 9** P.W. Botha, later Prime Minister of South Africa, 1978–89, speaking as Minister of Defence in 1977

*66 Russia is out to dominate Europe. She wants to control the destiny of Africa, for its raw materials and the sea route round the Cape. Russia is expanding her navy faster than any country in history and that can only mean she wants to dominate the seas. If you want to dominate the seas you must be able to control the South Atlantic and the Indian Ocean. The moment she succeeds in either of these Russia will concentrate on isolating America from Europe. 99*

S**OURCE 10** An extract from a South African government publication, 1982

*66 Should a Soviet puppet government ever be installed in Pretoria the Soviet Union would by this action grasp the perfect instrument for destroying the industrial and technological supremacy of the West. 99*

## ■ TASK

The South African government successfully used a mixture of financial incentives and Cold War propaganda to win support for apartheid in Britain, the USA, Germany, Japan and elsewhere. (Visiting Japanese business executives were declared 'honorary whites' by the South African government.) Western politicians and business people tended to use three explanations for their failure to support sanctions:

■ it was better to talk to the South Africans and try to persuade them gently to change
■ South Africa would gradually abandon apartheid as it got richer

■ sanctions would hit poor blacks harder than rich whites, so making the situation worse.

1. What arguments would you use to oppose each of the three statements?
2. Why was South African government propaganda so successful?
3. Complete the second row of the table on page 95 to show how the response of South Africa and the rest of the world affected the effectiveness of sanctions.

# 3. Protests by ordinary people

So far we have looked at what action governments could have taken against apartheid. But many ordinary people in Europe and the USA were opposed to apartheid. The shootings at Sharpeville in 1960 and the Rivonia Trial in 1965 caused outrage and a determination to do something.

### The International Defence and Aid Fund (IDAF)

This was set up in Britain in 1965 by a priest, Canon John Collins. It collected money to help the opponents of apartheid; it paid for lawyers to defend people put on trial for peaceful opposition and gave money to the families of those imprisoned. It tried to counter the propaganda coming out of South Africa. After the ANC had been banned and exiled, the IDAF worked with Oliver Tambo to promote the cause of peaceful opposition to apartheid.

**SOURCE 11** Canon Collins explained to the UN what the IDAF was trying to do, in June 1965

     *I think that as well as bringing aid to the persecuted victims of unjust laws and oppressive procedures, and relief to families, the IDAF has played a vital role in bringing about political change. And of much more importance, in my opinion, is that the contribution of IDAF fosters the morale of internal resistance. For, if the necessary political changes are to be brought about with the minimum of violence – and no sane person would wish it otherwise – it is the resistance movement inside South Africa which can give South Africa the ability to become a non-racial society based on a free and democratic way of life.*

**SOURCE 12** Canon Collins, speaking at the UN in August 1966

     *Dr Verwoerd and his colleagues would like the world to believe that South Africa is one of the bastions of Christian and Western civilisation. But the Defence and Aid Fund has so exposed the activities of the South African Special Branch that the government [of South Africa] has tried to ban it.*

### The Anti-Apartheid Movement

Organisations were formed in several countries of groups of people opposed to apartheid. One of the earliest was started in Sweden in 1959. The Swedish government was opposed to apartheid and worked directly to support the ANC, including giving grants of money. The British Anti-Apartheid Movement had no support from the government. For historic reasons (which you have read about in Chapter 1), Britain had closer links with South Africa than other countries, not only in business and finance, but also in sport.

Many white South Africans were passionate about sport, especially cricket and rugby. They applied apartheid throughout their sporting activities and this led to South Africa being banned from the Olympics in 1963. Threats from the Anti-Apartheid Movement stopped the summer 1970 cricket tour of England, but in autumn 1970 the South African rugby team came to Britain. The Anti-Apartheid Movement set up a special 'Stop the Seventy Tour Campaign' to disrupt the matches. Tin-tacks were thrown on to the pitch and several matches were abandoned. It was the last time a South African sports team played in Britain until 1996. Some British teams continued to tour South Africa, but eventually these visits stopped too. Sporting isolation hit keen South African sports fans almost more than other sanctions.

**SOURCE 13** Demonstrators squat around the coach carrying the South African rugby team, London 1969

**S**OURCE 14 Anti-apartheid demonstrators outside Barclay's Bank protesting about the loans being made to South Africa, 1978

**S**OURCE 15 Many items like these were produced to support the anti-apartheid campaign

**S**OURCE 16 An extract from the Barclays Bank Shadow Report, 1984. This annual report, first published by anti-apartheid campaigners in 1981, followed a similar format to official company reports but detailed how the bank's activities had helped sustain apartheid

*66 Barclays has helped finance the export of arms from Britain to South Africa. Documentary evidence has revealed that the bank's South African subsidiary provided a credit for a $108,000 rifle sale to the Pretoria authorities, although Barclays headquarters in London says that its South African subsidiary was unaware that the goods involved were arms . . .*

*Barclays continues to be a major source of foreign loans for South African state corporations. These . . . loans have new importance now that it is increasingly likely that International Monetary Fund assistance to South Africa will be cut off. 99*

The Anti-Apartheid Movement turned its attention to the British government, calling for trade boycotts of South Africa. Many British people refused to buy South African goods such as fruit and wine. Demonstrations were held outside the offices of British companies which invested in South Africa or which had factories or branches there. Students boycotted Barclays Bank because it was heavily involved in South Africa. People also held demonstrations outside the South African Embassy in London and kept up contacts with the exiled ANC.

In the USA a black trade unionist on the board of General Motors worked out a code of principles, called the Sullivan Principles, for the 340 US firms operating in South Africa. The code included equal pay for the same work, fair holidays, fairness in promotion and other measures designed to ensure equality at work for all South African employees, regardless of their colour.

4. What were the differences between the IDAF and the Anti-Apartheid Movement?
5. Why was the Anti-Apartheid Movement more successful in stopping sporting links with South Africa than in ending trade and business links?
6. What kinds of action can ordinary people carry out which governments cannot do?
7. Do you think government action was going to be necessary before apartheid could be overthrown?

### ■ ACTIVITY

It is 1978. You are a member of the local branch of the Anti-Apartheid Movement (AAM).

1. Make a report on what the AAM has done in the last few years, explaining:
a) which actions have been effective
b) which actions have not been effective.
2. What actions do you recommend your members carry out in future?

### ■ TASK

1. Complete the final row of the table on page 95, explaining what effect the various factors had on the efforts of ordinary people to resist apartheid.
2. From the information in your table, which do you think were the **three** most important reasons why apartheid survived?

# chapter 7

# WHY WAS APARTHEID COLLAPSING BY 1989?

## Introduction

IN 1978, AFTER 30 years, apartheid seemed safe, despite all the efforts described in Chapters 5 and 6 to remove it. But South Africa's white rulers had problems to face:

■ the threat of invasion from another country
■ international sanctions
■ the danger of internal uprising.

At the end of this chapter you are going to write an essay about why apartheid was collapsing by 1989. This chapter covers each of the three points here in turn and so will help you with your essay. Which of the three do you think will turn out to be the most important?

In 1978 the 'Muldergate' scandal (see page 97) led to the fall of Prime Minister John Vorster and showed that Nationalist politicians were not as virtuous as they liked to pretend. The man who stepped into this situation was P.W. Botha, Prime Minister from 1978 and President from 1984–89. He was nicknamed 'the Crocodile' and had a fierce temper. He was determined to keep white control of South Africa.

White rule had come to an end in **Angola** and **Mozambique** in 1976.

In the **wider world**, there was an almost total sporting and artistic boycott of South Africa and increasing pressure for sanctions to isolate the country economically. Foreign businesses were under pressure to withdraw investments.

Inside South Africa:
• the black population was growing faster than the white population; barely one in eight of the population was white in 1980, compared with one in five in 1950
• despite apartheid's 'influx control' policies, more than half of all blacks now lived in towns
• black opposition seemed impossible to crush; sabotage attacks by MK guerrillas were increasing.

White rule in Rhodesia ended in 1980 and the country was renamed **Zimbabwe**, under black majority rule.

**Key**
☐ Countries under black rule
▨ Countries under white rule

**Results**
1. The 'buffer states' that had protected South Africa's borders were falling away. South Africa now had hostile neighbours, ready to support the ANC and provide bases for its armed wing, MK.
2. The original apartheid vision of an all-white South Africa, with a black population confined to rural 'homelands' was obviously not going to happen.

**S**OURCE 1 The political situation facing South Africa by 1980

## ■ ACTIVITY

You are one of P.W. Botha's advisers. It is 1978. He has asked for your ideas on how to keep white control of South Africa. On the basis of what you already know, what are you going to do to:

■ hold on to the support of white voters?
■ keep in with world leaders?
■ deal with black opposition inside South Africa?

Are you going to:

■ tough it out, not giving an inch on apartheid?
■ make some concessions?
■ abandon apartheid completely?

1. On your own copy of the table below, record what you think the impact of each approach would be on the three different groups of people.
2. Decide what you think Botha should do and write your advice to him as a brief report.

Refer back to your table as you read this chapter.

| | White voters | World leaders | Black opposition |
|---|---|---|---|
| Tough it out | | | |
| Make concessions | | | |
| Abandon apartheid | | | |

# Total onslaught, total strategy

Botha had a tough interpretation of South Africa's problems, and tough solutions. He called them: **total onslaught, total strategy**.

**TOTAL ONSLAUGHT**
South Africa was facing a ruthless onslaught from Communist forces supported by the USSR, operating both inside and outside the country.

P.W. Botha, Prime Minister of South Africa 1978–84, President 1984–89

**TOTAL STRATEGY**
South Africa would fight this onslaught totally – abroad, in southern Africa and inside South Africa – by every possible means: military, economic, psychological and political.

**1. State Security Council**
- Botha had been Minister of Defence for many years. He had good links with army generals, particularly the chief, General Malan. He set up a STATE SECURITY COUNCIL (SSC) in 1982, consisting of army generals and police chiefs. It had more influence over Botha than the politicians in his Cabinet.
- The SSC was supported by a system of local JOINT MANAGEMENT CENTRES, run by a local police chief or army brigadier. It was almost a parallel government.

**2. Armed forces**
- Botha greatly increased the size of the armed forces. Since 1972 every South African male had had to do nine months' military service. Botha increased this period to two years. Men could also be called up to do up to 720 days of additional service at regular intervals or times of emergency.
- Two hundred thousand schoolchildren went on regular camps run by the army and joined cadet forces; it was hard not to join.
- By 1981 the SOUTH AFRICAN DEFENCE FORCE (SADF) numbered over 250,000, with another 250,000 in reserve.

**3. Arms industry**
- There was a world boycott on selling arms to South Africa, so it set up its own arms industry, called ARMSCOR. It made guns, tanks, rocket launchers and many other kinds of weapon, often using parts and machines supplied by countries willing to break the boycott.
- Military spending rose from 700 million rand in 1974 to 3,000 million rand by 1981.

**RESULT: BOTHA WAS AT THE HEAD OF A MAJOR MILITARY POWER.**

**S**OURCE 2  How Botha increased the military strength of South Africa

# What was Botha's 'Total Strategy' for South Africa's neighbours?

**SOURCE 1** Botha makes clear his attitude to his neighbours

*66 We want to show them that we want peace in the region, we want to contribute and we can help. But we also want to show them that if we are refused we can destroy the whole of southern Africa. 99*

## ■ TASK 1

As you read about Botha's foreign policy, list the aspects which are:

1. about peace
2. about using force.

BOTHA'S FOREIGN POLICY is outlined in Source 1. He called it *dwangpostuur*, or 'threat posture'. It is an attitude of 'peace – or else'. As we saw on page 96, however much black African countries loathed apartheid and wanted to support the ANC, they were often economically dependent on South Africa and forced to stay on good terms with the government. They sent men to work in South African mines; they exported goods through South African ports. Botha played on these economic needs. South Africa's neighbours were too poor to think of challenging South Africa, particularly now that it was becoming a military superpower as well.

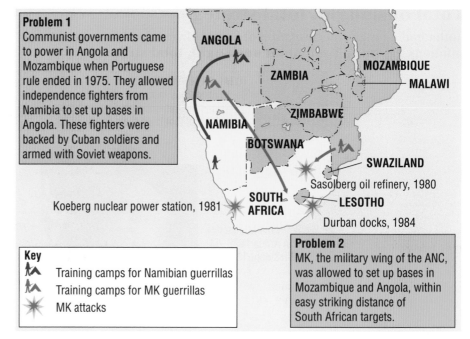

**Problem 1**
Communist governments came to power in Angola and Mozambique when Portuguese rule ended in 1975. They allowed independence fighters from Namibia to set up bases in Angola. These fighters were backed by Cuban soldiers and armed with Soviet weapons.

Koeberg nuclear power station, 1981
Sasolberg oil refinery, 1980
Durban docks, 1984

**Key**
- 𝄃 Training camps for Namibian guerrillas
- 𝄃 Training camps for MK guerrillas
- ✳ MK attacks

**Problem 2**
MK, the military wing of the ANC, was allowed to set up bases in Mozambique and Angola, within easy striking distance of South African targets.

**SOURCE 2** Problems facing the South African government in the late 1970s and early 1980s

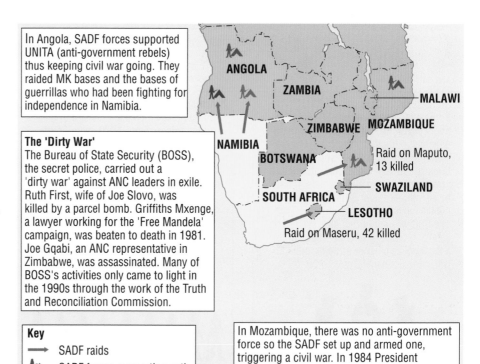

In Angola, SADF forces supported UNITA (anti-government rebels) thus keeping civil war going. They raided MK bases and the bases of guerrillas who had been fighting for independence in Namibia.

**The 'Dirty War'**
The Bureau of State Security (BOSS), the secret police, carried out a 'dirty war' against ANC leaders in exile. Ruth First, wife of Joe Slovo, was killed by a parcel bomb. Griffiths Mxenge, a lawyer working for the 'Free Mandela' campaign, was beaten to death in 1981. Joe Gqabi, an ANC representative in Zimbabwe, was assassinated. Many of BOSS's activities only came to light in the 1990s through the work of the Truth and Reconciliation Commission.

Raid on Maputo, 13 killed
Raid on Maseru, 42 killed

In Mozambique, there was no anti-government force so the SADF set up and armed one, triggering a civil war. In 1984 President Machel, under pressure to rebuild his country, made an agreement with South Africa not to assist the ANC. Nevertheless in 1986 his plane was deliberately misdirected by a South African beacon so that it crashed and he was killed.

**Key**
- → SADF raids
- 𝄃 SADF forces supporting anti-government rebels
- 𝄃 Namibian guerrilla camps
- 𝄃 MK guerrilla camps

**SOURCE 3** The South African government's response to the problems

**SOURCE 4** A fire caused by an MK bomb explosion at Sasolberg oil refinery, 1980. South Africa did not have its own oil reserves and was threatened by oil sanctions. At this experimental refinery government scientists were trying to find a way of using coal (of which South Africa had plenty) to make oil

**SOURCE 5** A casualty of an SADF air-strike on an ANC base in Mozambique, 1983

**SOURCE 6** In 1991 Foreign Minister Pik Botha admitted that South Africa had spent money to keep the civil war going in Namibia

*   Yes, yes, the South African government did provide funds ... In a quiet way, in a secret way, we assisted them ... The sum was considerable, well over 100 million rand.* **"**

# Psychological warfare

The other side of Botha's 'Total Strategy' for South Africa's neighbours was the psychological war. He put across the message that South Africa was fighting a war against Communism on behalf of democracy, freedom, Christianity and free enterprise. His soldiers seemed to be convinced by his message.

**SOURCE 7** Young white men at Pretoria University discuss doing their military service

*   **Jaap du Plessis**: We were actually fighting for Christianity, because Communism doesn't allow you to practise your own religion. Do you ever think about what the other side is fighting for?*
***James van Zyl***: *The terrorists are only the instruments that the Russians use to fight Christianity, so they can take over the world.*
***Benny Viviers***: *It is a Christian war. We are not the aggressors, they are the aggressors. We are only defending our property and our people.* **"**

**SOURCE 8** Sometimes the propaganda was a bit crude. These teenage girls describe a lecture at veld school, a compulsory weekend camp run by the army

*   **Debbie**: In veld school we did Communism, we did the South African flag, we did terrorism, and one whole lecture was about how sex, Communism and drugs all goes into the music we listen to.*
***Roseanne***: *I think it was too old-fashioned. I mean, listening to music doesn't automatically make you take drugs or have sex every night or become a Communist.* **"**

1. Read Source 7. It is true that many National Party leaders called themselves Christians. It is true that the USSR supplied some of the guerrillas and MK with weapons. Does that mean that these young men are describing the situation accurately?
2. Read Source 8. Why was Roseanne not convinced by what she was told?
3. These two sources are biased. How would you use them to find out about the situation in South Africa at this time?

## ■ TASK 2

How successful was Botha at dealing with the threat to South Africa from outside invasion: unsuccessful/fairly successful/very successful?
   Give reasons for your choice.

# What was Botha's 'Total Strategy' for Western leaders?

BY 1978 SOUTH Africa was part of the web of international trade. Wealthy South African whites had grown used to their Mercedes cars, their Italian fashions and their Japanese electronic goods. They needed Botha to persuade Western leaders to continue to trade with South Africa.

The United Nations, the Commonwealth and black South African leaders were stepping up their call for sanctions. Across the world, many ordinary people were answering, and putting pressure on their governments (see pages 100–1).

Botha's 'Total Strategy' for Western leaders was to play on their worries about the Communist threat as hard as he could. He was helped by two Western leaders who were in key positions for most of the 1980s: Ronald Reagan, President of the USA from 1980–88, and Margaret Thatcher, who was Prime Minister of Britain from 1979–90. Both were staunch anti-Communists. Neither liked principles to get in the way of trade and business. They were ready to hear what Botha told them about 'reform'. They strongly resisted the pressure for sanctions from the UN, the Commonwealth and their own peoples.

**SOURCE 1** Ronald Reagan and Margaret Thatcher, both strong supporters of South Africa and the apartheid regime

**SOURCE 2** US President Ronald Reagan, speaking in 1981

66 Can we abandon a country that has stood behind us in every war we've ever fought, a country that is strategically essential to the free world? It has production of minerals we must have. I just feel that if we are going to sit down at a table and negotiate with the Russians, then surely we can keep the door open and continue to negotiate with a friendly nation like South Africa. 99

1. What reasons does Reagan give for opposing sanctions against South Africa?
2. Which are:
a) reasons of principle?
b) reasons connected with US prosperity?

**SOURCE 3** Mrs Thatcher was still opposing sanctions in 1986

66 To me it is absurd that people should be prepared to put increasing power into the hands of the Soviet Union, on the grounds that they disapprove of apartheid in South Africa. 99

3. What does Mrs Thatcher agree with Reagan about?

**SOURCE 4** Oliver Tambo, leader of the ANC in exile, in 1986

66 The argument for sanctions is that such a massive blow would make it almost impossible for the present government to stay in power. The alternative is we will be left with nothing but to fight it out with everything we have. The consequence of this is too ghastly to contemplate. 99

**SOURCE 5** Desmond Tutu, the black Archbishop of Cape Town, called for sanctions in 1986

66 I have no hope of real change from this government unless they are forced. I call on the international community to apply punitive [very harsh] sanctions against this government to help us establish a new South Africa – non-racial, democratic, participatory [involving everyone] and just. This is a non-violent strategy to help us do so. There is a great deal of goodwill still in our country between races. We can live together as one people, one family, black and white together. 99

4. Compare Sources 4 and 5. On what do they agree?
5. How do they differ?
6. Can you explain these differences?

# What was Botha's 'Total Strategy' for South Africa?

A S WELL AS being close to the army chiefs, Botha was also close to the leaders of big business in South Africa. They had always criticised Verwoerd's apartheid because it did not meet their needs, as Source 1 explains.

## Big businesses and farmers needed ...

A steady supply of reasonably satisfied workers for their factories ...

BUT black workers found it hard to move to cities and were harassed and resentful when they got there.

Skilled workers for their modern, complex machines ...

BUT black children were poorly educated and learned few of the skills needed.

People in South Africa with enough money to buy their goods ...

BUT most blacks were so poor they could barely afford basic necessities.

Fewer unskilled farm workers because big farms were now mechanised ...

BUT black people were tied to the land.

S OURCE 1 How apartheid was failing to meet the needs of big businesses and farmers in the 1970s

## ■ ACTIVITY

Look at Source 1. You are one of Prime Minister Botha's advisers. It is 1978. What do you think should happen to apartheid policies in future?

■ Do you think there should be changes? If so, how will they affect white support for apartheid? What will people abroad think?
■ Do you think things should stay as they are? If so, how will that affect big businesses? What will the reaction be from abroad?

Write a report for the Prime Minister and advise him on what to do.

Botha offered to reform apartheid. Early apartheid had assumed that blacks were simple, rural people, unfitted for city life; only outside 'agitators' and Communists made them demand human rights. Now Botha assumed that blacks were simple people who just wanted to be a bit better off. His reforms were designed to support the demands of big business by removing some of apartheid's petty restrictions and unfairness, and also to create a new black middle class. That way whites would remain in control but enough blacks would have a stake in the system to blunt the force of black protest. Botha described this policy as 'Winning Hearts and Minds' (WHAM).

These changes had two aims:

■ to give South African business leaders the kind of workforce and consumers they had been asking for, and
■ to be able to tell the outside world that reforms were taking place.

In this way, Botha hoped that whites would be able to hang on to power.

## Botha's reforms

A number of investigations were carried out into possible reforms of apartheid and Botha put most of the resulting ideas into practice.

### ■ TASK 1

1. On your own copy of this table note down how each of the six reforms shown opposite was designed to meet one of the demands of big business or the outside world.

| | 1. Trade unions | 2. Living in cities | 3. Job reservation | 4. Schools | 5. Power sharing | 6. Petty apartheid |
|---|---|---|---|---|---|---|
| More skilled, contented workers | | | | | | |
| Better-educated workers | | | | | | |
| More black consumers | | | | | | |
| Less need for unskilled farm workers | | | | | | |
| World opinion | | | | | | |

2. In 1979, Dr Koornhof, Botha's Minister of Co-operation and Development, said in the USA: 'Apartheid as you have known it is dead.' What **three** points might he have made to support this statement?
3. Look back to the table about apartheid that you completed in Chapter 4 (page 63, Task 2). Make **three** statements to contradict Koornhof's claim.

### ■ TASK 2

Think about the six South Africans below:

a) a skilled black factory worker
b) a black farm worker
c) a black school pupil aged 14
d) a Coloured woman
e) a white worker
f) a white business person.

Look at Botha's reforms shown opposite. How would each of these people react to each reform? Which of the changes would they like, or dislike, most?

### 1. Trade unions

The Wiehahn Report (1979) recommended that trade unions for black workers – banned since the 1960s – should be legalised. This may seem strange, but businesses had suffered from sudden 'wildcat' strikes in the 1970s, when secret, illegal unions had sprung up. Wiehahn argued that legal unions would act more responsibly and white employers would know who they needed to negotiate with, as in the USA and most European countries.

**SOURCE 2** P.W. Botha, speaking in 1986

*❝ We hope to create a middle class among the nations of South Africa. Because if a man has possessions and is able to build his family life around those possessions, then one has clearly laid the foundation for resisting Communism. If anyone has something to protect, to keep as his own, then he fights Communism more readily. ❞*

### 2. Job reservation

Jobs previously reserved for whites were opened up.

### 3. Schools

The Lange Report (1981) recommended that a single education system be set up (black education was currently under the Ministry of *Bantu* Affairs) and more spent on black education. Botha was not prepared to do the first of these, but spending on black education tripled through the 1980s.

## 4. Living in cities

The Reikert Report of 1979 recommended that blacks should be allowed to move around the country more freely and buy houses. This did not mean, of course, that they could live in 'white' areas, but they could move to black townships and buy houses there – if they could afford them. The influx control laws were relaxed; so were the laws on blacks owning property in urban areas.

Botha and his friends in big business got together in an organisation called the Urban Foundation to build new, better, houses in black townships.

Advertisements began to focus on this new, wealthy, black middle class.

**SOURCE 3** Richard Maponya, a black millionaire who has made his fortune by opening up a chain of grocery stores in the black townships

**SOURCE 4** From the commentary given to a bus tour for foreign journalists by David Thebehli, Chairman of the Community Council of Soweto, 1980

❝ Ladies and gentlemen, we're coming now to Selection Park, the new area where elite housing is in progress. Now the average price of these houses varies from 15,000 rand to 28,000 rand. They are two and three-bedroomed houses and they're built according to the same standards as any middle-class European home. They are fully serviced with electricity, water and sewerage and there will be tarred streets here as well. ❞

**SOURCE 5** A declaration by P.W. Botha

❝ I'm giving you a final warning: one man, one vote in this country is out – that is never! ❞

## 5. Power sharing

In 1983 a new constitution was devised for South Africa. It was complicated, but Coloureds and Indians were to be allowed to vote for their own representatives in their own parliaments. There would be 178 places in the whites' parliament; 85 in the Coloureds' parliament and 45 in the parliament for Indians. A new Cabinet would be drawn from these parliaments, also in the same numerical proportions. Blacks were not to take part, but local elected black assemblies were to take over running some local affairs. (See also Source 1, page 114.)

## 6. Petty apartheid

The Mixed Marriages Act of 1949 was REPEALED. Local government, which was responsible for putting into practice the Separate Amenities Act of 1953, was encouraged to desegregate parks, shops and other public amenities. Pass Laws were relaxed and eventually abolished altogether in 1986.

**SOURCE 6** The beach at Durban after the end of apartheid restrictions

MOST WHITES SUPPORTED Botha's policies and the changes he wanted. Under his leadership, the National Party won the 1981 and 1987 elections with huge majorities. However, he faced continuing opposition from blacks and from some whites.

## White opposition

Some whites were horrified at what they saw as the abandonment of apartheid. Botha made little effort to win their support and merely snarled at them that they must 'adapt or die'. White workers had lost the security offered to them by the policy of job reservation; small farmers were losing black labourers to the cities. In 1982 Dr Treurnicht led eighteen National MPs out of the National Party in protest and formed the Conservative Party. It did not really threaten the National Party rule, but in the 1987 elections, 37 per cent of Afrikaners did not support the National Party. The unity of Afrikaners behind the National Party, built up to win power from the English-speakers in 1948, was over.

Even further to the right than the Conservatives was the Afrikaner Weerstandsbeweging (AWB). This resistance movement, with its Nazi-style uniforms and crude racism, was apparently ready to fight for white supremacy.

**SOURCE 1** COSATU's second trade union congress

## Black opposition

### 1. Trade unions

Trade union leaders took advantage of their new legal status to win wide support among black workers. They began to take militant industrial action. In 1974 14,167 working days were lost through strikes; in 1982 365,337 days were lost. Strong leaders emerged, such as Cyril Ramaphosa, of the black National Union of Mineworkers. They joined together in the Confederation of South African Trade Unions (COSATU), see Source 1. COSATU leaders realised that, with no legal, political, mass organisations for black people, trade unions could step into the gap and act on a whole range of black grievances. In return, many strikes had wide community support. Striking workers were supported by the black community in total boycotts of the shops or goods of the company the unions were striking against.

**SOURCE 2** A demonstration by members of the students' organisation COSAS

## 2. Schools

By 1980 half the black people in South Africa were under 25 years old. The slight increases in education spending in Botha's reforms did not even cover the rising number wanting to go to school, and, once there, to stay on into secondary school. Students were fed up with huge classes, poorly-qualified teachers, no books and no future in a white-run system. The children had also seen that it was possible for them to take the lead, during the Soweto school riots of 1976 (see pages 88–90). They could see the links between their problems and other grievances in their communities: all suffered from apartheid in different ways.

In 1979 the Congress of South African Students (COSAS) was formed (see Source 2). In 1980–81 nearly 100,000 school pupils and university students boycotted classes in protest against conditions. They also made links with other groups and COSAS joined in rent strikes and consumer boycotts.

## 3. Squatters

The loosening of apartheid's influx control policies meant that blacks flocked to the cities. The housing situation became desperate. Huge new squatter camps grew up, like Crossroads near Cape Town. These new camps were regularly bulldozed by the Ministry of Co-operation and Development. By the mid-1980s, following international pressure, new settlements were being built.

A tiny number of black people benefited from the reforms. But the great majority saw little or no change in their lives under Botha's WHAM policy.

## ■ ACTIVITY

Work in pairs. It is 1984 and you are members of the Board of Directors of a British company heavily involved in South Africa. You are under pressure from anti-apartheid activists to pull out of South Africa.

- One of you supports Botha's reforms and puts forward all the points in favour of staying in South Africa.
- The other puts forward all the points against Botha's reforms being effective.

After you have discussed the two views, make a decision about whether you are going to keep your business in South Africa or not. Then:

a) write a memo to the rest of the Board explaining why you have reached this decision, dealing with the arguments on the other side, or,
b) explain your decision to the rest of the class.

# **H**ow did black Church leaders oppose apartheid?

WITH LEADERS SUCH as Nelson Mandela and Walter Sisulu in prison on Robben Island, and others in exile, like Oliver Tambo, or dead, like Steve Biko, blacks needed new leaders to speak about their grievances against the flood of white propaganda. The few organisations that could speak for black South Africans were their Churches. Black Church leaders got involved in protest through their concern for the lives of their people and because they saw apartheid as fundamentally unchristian. These leaders included Allan Boesak (see page 115) and Frank Chikane. Frank Chikane was detained by police four times between 1978 and 1982. In 1981 he was sacked by the small white-run church to which he belonged.

**S**OURCE 1  Frank Chikane

Most well-known of all was the Anglican priest Desmond Tutu. Tutu became General Secretary of the South African Council of Churches in 1978. From this position he used his abilities as a speaker to denounce apartheid. He became famous worldwide and won the Nobel Peace Prize in 1984. In 1985 he was made Bishop of Johannesburg and in 1986 Archbishop of Cape Town, head of the Anglican Church in South Africa.

**S**OURCE 2  Desmond Tutu

**SOURCE 3** Back in 1976 Tutu wrote to Prime Minister John Vorster

*I am writing to you, sir, because I have a growing nightmarish fear that unless something drastic is done very soon then bloodshed and violence are going to happen in South Africa . . .*

*How long can a people bear such blatant injustice and suffering? Much of the white community, with all its prosperity, its privilege, its beautiful homes, its servants, its leisure, is hag-ridden by fear and insecurity. And this will continue until South Africans of all races are free. Freedom, sir, is indivisible. The whites in this land will not be free until all sections of our community are genuinely free.*

**SOURCE 4** Tutu's reaction to the 1983 constitution

*There was a road sign which said: 'Careful, natives cross here' and someone changed it to read 'Careful, natives very cross here'. Perhaps that sums it all up. The natives of this beautiful country, the indigenous inhabitants [not descended from settlers], the sons and daughters of this black soil are very angry. Blacks are expected to exercise their political ambitions in unviable, poverty-stricken, arid Bantustan homelands, ghettos of misery, inexhaustible reservoirs of cheap black labour. Blacks are systematically being stripped of their citizenship and turned into aliens in the land of their birth. This is apartheid's 'final solution', just as Nazism had its final solution for the Jews in Hitler's Aryan madness.*

**SOURCE 5** In this sermon from 1989 he showed up the ridiculousness of apartheid

*What does the colour of a person's skin tell you about that person? Does it tell you if that person is intelligent? Does the colour of a person's skin tell you that person is loving? Supposing we said that the thing that determines privilege is the size of your nose. Now I have a large nose, and I say now 'Ah! You want to go to the toilet; that toilet is reserved for people with large noses; if you have a small nose you are in trouble now . . . That university, you enter only if you have a large nose like mine. If you have a small nose then you must apply to the Minister of Small Nose Affairs for permission to attend the university for large noses.*

**SOURCE 6** In this letter to Botha in 1988 Tutu destroys the claim that apartheid has any biblical justification

*The Bible teaches us that what invests [gives] each person with infinite value is not this or that arbitrarily chosen biological attribute, but that each person is created in the image of God. Apartheid, the policy of your government, claims that what makes a person qualify for privilege and political power is that biological irrelevance, the colour of a person's skin. That is clearly at variance with the teaching of the Bible and the teaching of Our Lord and Saviour Jesus Christ. Hence the Church's criticism that your apartheid policies are not only unjust and oppressive. They are positively unbiblical, unchristian, immoral and evil.*

**SOURCE 7** Tutu also called for the release of Nelson Mandela

*We are not calling for his release on humanitarian grounds. We are doing so on political grounds. We are saying he is our leader. He is the acknowledged leader of the group most blacks support, but more than that, we are saying he is symbolic because we want all leaders, all political prisoners, released, not on humanitarian grounds, but on the grounds that this is how we build up a climate in which we can start to talk.*

In his speeches, sermons and letters Tutu used jokes, passion, the Bible and a sound understanding of people's lives to show up the wickedness of apartheid and proclaim his vision of a multiracial South Africa – 'a rainbow-coloured people', as he called them.

1. Find examples in these sources of:
a) humour
b) non-violence
c) references to the Bible.
2. In Source 3 Tutu says that freedom is indivisible, that the whites are not free. What does he mean? Is he right?
3. In Source 7, he calls for the release of Nelson Mandela, but not 'on humanitarian grounds', that is, not because his imprisonment is cruel. Why does Tutu want Mandela released?
4. What is Tutu's aim for South Africa?
5. How is this going to be achieved?

# What form did opposition to the new constitution take?

## ■ TASK

By 1985 Botha's policies were clearly not working. As you find out in the next four pages what was going wrong, use your own copy of this table to record some of the reasons why.

|  | Example | Mark out of ten for importance | Reason for mark |
|---|---|---|---|
| Non-violent opposition |  |  |  |
| Violent opposition |  |  |  |
| International protests |  |  |  |

1. In the second column, give an example of each type of action.
2. In the third column, give a mark out of ten for how important you think it was.
3. Give reasons for the mark you have awarded in the final column.

IT WAS OPPOSITION to the new constitution of 1983 which first of all united the different protest groups together and then triggered a nationwide mass protest movement. Botha's so-called 'reforms' had made black people angry. They actually offered no improvement at all to the great mass of the black African population. Now blacks were completely excluded from the new constitution. Coloureds and Indians were just as angry: it did not take much skill at arithmetic to see that the whites would be still in

## The UDF

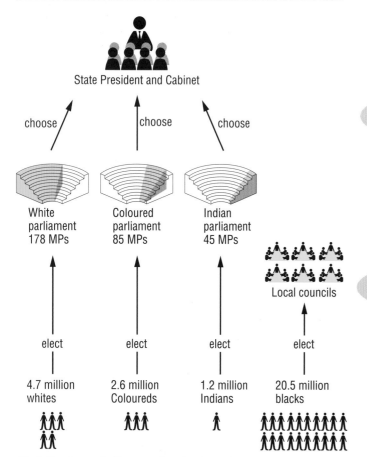

Students and school pupil groups, such as COSAS

Trade unions

Church groups

State President and Cabinet

choose ↑    choose ↑    choose ↑

White parliament 178 MPs

Coloured parliament 85 MPs

Indian parliament 45 MPs

Local councils

↑ elect    ↑ elect    ↑ elect    ↑ elect

4.7 million whites

2.6 million Coloureds

1.2 million Indians

20.5 million blacks

**SOURCE 1** A diagram showing how Botha's new power-sharing constitution was supposed to work

complete control of the country, while posing to the outside world as multiracialists.

Blacks, Coloureds and Indians decided that the best form of protest was to boycott the elections to the new parliaments and local councils. That would show the world that the changes had no backing from the people. A new organisation was needed to co-ordinate the protest. This was the United Democratic Front, the UDF.

Women's groups

Civic groups, that is, local people who had joined together to deal with a specific local problem, such as bus fares, or refuse collection

Indian community organisations

**S**OURCE 2  Frank Chikane at the launch of the UDF in 1983. The UDF was made up of 565 other local or special organisations, mainly of the types shown here

**S**OURCE 3  Allan Boesak, President of the World Alliance of Reformed Churches and a university chaplain

**S**OURCE 4  Allan Boesak, speaking in 1983

    **66** *Let me remind you of three little words. The first word is 'all'. We want all our rights, not just a few token handouts which the government sees fit to give ... And we want all of South Africa's people to have their rights, not just a selected few, not just Coloureds or Indians.*

*    The second word is the word 'here'. We want all our rights here in a united, undivided South Africa. We do not want them in impoverished homelands, we do not want them in our separate 'group areas'.*

*    The third word is the word 'now'. We want all our rights, we want them here and we want them now. We have been waiting so long. We have been struggling so long. We have pleaded, cried, petitioned too long now. We have been jailed, exiled, killed for too long. Now is the time.* **99**

1. What are the 'three little words'? Explain why each was important to the UDF.
2. On the evidence of this speech, would Allan Boesak be a supporter of the ANC Freedom Charter (see page 70)?

**115**

## The boycott campaign, 1983–84

The UDF campaign was well organised in comparison with the ANC campaigns of the 1950s. The UDF produced leaflets and posters and organised door-to-door visits. But the ideals that it proclaimed were the same as those of the ANC: the Freedom Charter and a democratic, non-racial South Africa. ANC activists like Albertina Sisulu, wife of Walter Sisulu and a veteran campaigner in her own right, played a big part in the UDF. From now on there was a huge revival of interest in the ANC and increasing calls for the release of its president, Nelson Mandela, from prison.

When it came to voting for the new parliaments and local black councils, the boycott was very successful. In the elections of August 1984 only 29 per cent of Coloureds and 19 per cent of Indians actually voted. The boycott of elections to local black councils produced a 21 per cent turnout; in some places it was far lower: the man 'elected' mayor of Soweto, which had a population of 2 million, received just 1,115 votes.

## The Vaal Triangle uprising, 1984–85

The Vaal Triangle is the area of black townships to the south of Johannesburg. The protests started with a school boycott in September 1984. The protestors' demands included a ban on unqualified teachers, access to free books and paper, an end to excessive corporal punishment and an end to sexual harassment. In some towns COSAS students had helped local trade unions with disputes, so now the unions helped the students with strikes, known as stay-at-homes.

The white government had given the new black councils the task of putting up rents, at a time of distress and 30 per cent unemployment, so the councils were unpopular from the beginning. They were also often corrupt. In some places they had links with the local taxi firms on whom local people depended to get to work. Elsewhere the councillors gave out liquor licences to each other. In both cases the councillors seemed to be more interested in using their position to make money for themselves and their cronies than in helping their people.

**S**OURCE 5  A black woman is set upon by police during the Vaal Triangle uprising

There were rent strikes. In some places councillors' houses were burnt. The police called on the army for help. SADF forces began to operate in the townships, stopping people to see their passes and arresting them. Soon there were shootings: the army killed young protesters. Violence escalated and spread to other parts of South Africa. In spite of their efforts, the police and army never regained full control of the townships.

The remarkable thing about the uprising was that it was led by children. In the town of Tumahole, Stompie Moeketsie, aged 13 in 1987, led an army of 1,500 under-14s who burnt down the Town Hall. He was the youngest person to be detained under the State of Emergency (see pages 118–121). Source 7 gives another example, from Sharpeville.

**S**OURCE 6  Stompie Moeketsie

**S**OURCE 7  Petrus Tom, a black adult, describes the opening of the uprising in Sharpeville on 3 September 1984

66 *Everybody was at home. The children made road blocks and burnt houses. They took old cars and burning tyres and blocked the street. The children decided to go to the administration offices. They said everybody must go to the administration offices. They were singing – a lot of children.*

*I found the hippos [armoured personnel carriers] standing at the administration offices with soldiers and television cameras. They said we could only send delegates to talk to them. People were delegated by the children to demand that we pay 30 rand and no more. When the delegates returned without an answer, they said, 'Well, as long as you haven't an answer, we're going to stand here.'*

*The older people advised the children that it was dangerous to confront these people like this because we knew what happened in 1960 when we were facing the police like this and they opened fire. The children said 'No, this is not 1960, this is 1984. You can't talk about what happened in 1960. What we are doing is different from that'* 99

3.  What examples are there in Source 7 of the children taking the lead in protest?
4.  What were the children's grievances?
5.  How does this source show the children going beyond their grievances at school?

## Financial crisis, 1985

On its TV screens the whole world watched the events taking place on the streets of South Africa. Business leaders who had believed that Botha would make reform work changed their minds. Barclays sold their South African banks. Other businesses gave way to years of pressure from their shareholders and pulled out. Important South African business leaders arranged a meeting with the ANC.

Botha's last chance was a speech he was due to make on 15 August 1985. It was hoped he would announce more reforms, break through the deadlock, perhaps even release Nelson Mandela. Instead he simply talked tough. US bankers had had enough. The international value of the rand dropped by 35 per cent. The South African Stock Exchange was closed. The huge military forces Botha had built up were expensive and taxes had to be put up to pay for them. White South Africans felt the pinch: their incomes fell sharply. They could not travel or buy goods abroad so easily. At last sanctions had begun to bite.

Botha had nothing more to say or to offer to South Africa. He had tried his 'Total Strategy' and it had failed. He was not prepared to try another route.

# What happened during the State of Emergency, 1985–90?

IN 1985 BOTHA declared a State of Emergency. This gave his government sweeping powers: it was virtually military rule. Soldiers could arrest anyone, interrogate anyone, search anywhere, close buildings, stop meetings. Newspapers were heavily censored so that only government press releases could be published. In an effort to force them to go back to school, children were not allowed outside by day. Twenty-five thousand UDF members were detained. At least as many more went into hiding.

SOURCE 1 The censored front page of the *Weekly Mail*, 1988

SOURCE 2 Muslim leader Moulana Faried Essack tries to stop police from removing the ANC flag from the coffin of an MK member, 1987

**SOURCE 3** A Soweto mother interviewed about her son

*❝ SOWETO MOTHER: At first I felt very bitter, but now I am with my son in every step he is taking.*
***Interviewer:** What are those steps?*
***SM:** He is following the rest of the people of this country who are fighting in the struggle. That is why he left.*
***Interviewer:** Do you feel he will succeed?*
***SM:** Well, I can't say, because some of them don't succeed. When they come back they are shot or put in jail. But he is a freedom fighter. On that point I stand with him.*
***Interviewer:** You call him a freedom fighter. To the government he's a terrorist.*
***SM:** I don't understand why they are called terrorists because they are not terrorising anybody – they are fighting for our rights. I think they have resorted to violence because so many times they sent people to try to talk but nothing was done. We blacks, we are just kept like children, who are told what to do, where to go, how far to go. We cannot even talk freely. I think our children are on the right track. ❞*

**SOURCE 4** Desmond Tutu kept up the pressure for non-violent resistance to apartheid, as this extract from a 1989 speech shows

*❝ You have no option but to be involved in this struggle. I call on you to know that it is God's struggle. You say, but you will get into trouble. Of course! Whoever saw powerful people give up their power without doing anything? The powerful will get angry. Well, so what is new? I invite you to come into this enterprise, God's enterprise, to change this country, to make this country what it is going to become: a land where all, black, white, green, whatever, will be able to hold hands together.*

*I call on you young people especially. I know that you are frustrated many, many times. You try to be non-violent and even this provokes violence. But that is precisely because they have nothing else. They have power but they have no authority, no moral authority. ❞*

**SOURCE 5** A lone Soweto woman protests as SADF forces move into the township, 1985

SOURCE 6 SADF soldiers with a 'hippo' armoured vehicle,1986

## Violence between black groups

As well as violence between protesters and troops, there was violence between black groups. Blacks who were thought to be working with the government were killed. These included councillors and black policemen. 'Comrades', as the anti-government groups called themselves, began 'necklace' killings, in which a used car tyre was filled with petrol, forced over the victim's body and set alight. This led to retaliation killings as people turned on their attackers. Gangs of black 'vigilantes', as they were called, were hired by the police as 'instant constables' (*kitskonstabels*) and attacked anti-government groups (see Source 8). Squatter houses at Crossroads were destroyed nightly by young gangs. In Natal violence broke out between ANC supporters and those who supported Inkatha, the Zulu organisation led by Chief Buthelezi (see Chapter 8 for more information on this development).

SOURCE 8 Romeo Mbambo describes how government officials hired him to kill 'comrades'

*66 We would be called to meet officials. Then, names of the people to be eliminated would be given to us. Then we'd be given equipment, firearms, explosives, everything. Then we'd go and carry out those orders, just like that. 99*

SOURCE 9 A victim of a 'necklace' killing

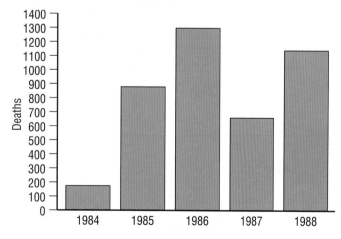

SOURCE 7 Deaths in political violence, 1984–88

By 1989 South Africa was descending into chaos. The ANC had given the order: 'Make South Africa ungovernable'. They had almost succeeded: the South African government could not re-establish control over the black townships. People's courts dealt with disorder. People's schools were set up as black students and children attempted to repair their missing education, under the COSAS slogan 'Each one teach one!' But the revolutionaries could not overthrow the government because the army and the police were too strong. It was deadlock.

Botha had run out of ideas. He became ill and was voted out of power. The future seemed to be only a long and bloody war.

### ■ TALKING POINTS

The ANC had called on its members to 'make South Africa ungovernable'.

1. What evidence is there that they were succeeding?
2. What do you think happened next?

### ■ TASK

At the beginning of this chapter we saw that the main threats to white rule in South Africa came from:

- invasion from outside
- international sanctions
- uprising from within.

Use the work you have done for the Tasks on pages 105, 108 and 114 to help you write an essay to answer this question: Why was apartheid collapsing by 1989? Your teacher will give you a sheet to help you to plan your answer.

**SOURCE 10** The growing chaos in South Africa and the hopelessness felt by black teachers and students in schools in the black townships is shown in this description of exam week in a Soweto school in 1989. The reporter, from the *Johannesburg Weekly Mail*, shows up the disorganised state of Botha's administration

66 *I was taken by a teacher to a Standard Seven classroom where an exam was in progress. The room had no electricity and was dark. The light fitting hung dangerously loose. As I entered, a pair of twins were leaving. They were going home, they told the exasperated teacher, because they couldn't read what was written on the exam paper. I saw plenty of such papers where the typing or printing was so bad that they were illegible. While I watched, another teacher arrived to try to clarify mistakes in the Standard Seven Sotho paper. 'I cannot read question six, so speed up, kids. Move to top gear and skip it. Well, let's see question seven. If you haven't studied any of the books or poems in this question, skip it 'cause you can't answer it.' By the end of the day the register had still not been taken.* 99

### ■ TALKING POINT

Source 9 is a shocking picture. I have included it because I think you ought to see exactly what the results of necklacing were – after all, the person shown here was not an isolated case. The frequent horrific murders carried out in this way were an important background to the peace-making process. But suppose this person was your sister? Your father? Would you want her or his dead body displayed in a textbook for all to see? What do you think?

# HOW DID APARTHEID END?

## **H**ow did South Africa change when de Klerk became President?

AT THE END of the 1980s, I, like many other people, thought that South Africa was heading for a bloodbath. There seemed no solution to the conflict except through a war, which would certainly be a vicious one. Yet in 1994 this picture, Source 1, was taken: as a result of a free election, in which all races took part, a black President was elected, with a mixed-race Cabinet. How had this come about?

The man who took over as President after Botha was F.W. de Klerk. De Klerk did not seem like someone who would change much. Born in 1938, the son of a leading National Party politician, he was a lifelong National Party member and a strong believer in racial separation. Yet in his first speech to Parliament in February 1990 he set out drastic changes:

- he unbanned the ANC, the PAC and the SACP
- he announced the release of Nelson Mandela and his fellow prisoners
- he said he was going to work towards equal rights for all South Africans.

In half an hour he abandoned years of apartheid policies.

**SOURCE 1** Nelson Mandela, President of South Africa 1994–99, at his inauguration

**SOURCE 2** F.W. de Klerk, President of South Africa 1989–94

122

# Why did de Klerk abandon apartheid?

**1.** He had to do something to bring South Africa back to a situation of law and order. It was on the verge of civil war and the government could not regain full control.

**2.** The South African economy was in deep trouble and would only get worse if things just drifted.

**3.** The National Party was losing support. It won a majority in the 1989 elections, but got less than 50 per cent of the vote. The Conservative Party, which opposed Botha's attempts to change apartheid, was the biggest opposition party.

**4.** De Klerk was very religious and believed God had called him to lead South Africa to a new future.

**5.** The Cold War had ended with a peace treaty between the USA and the USSR in 1987 and the destruction of the Berlin Wall in 1989. There was now no danger from an international Soviet threat.

**6.** National Party officials had had secret meetings with ANC leaders in England and Switzerland. They were impressed by the people they met and reported that the ANC was willing to talk.

**7.** The ANC might not do that well once it had been unbanned. Perhaps the National Party could hold on to power by working with other black organisations such as the Inkatha Freedom Party.

**8.** A power-sharing arrangement might be made, in which whites hung on to power, rather than elections on a one person, one vote system, which would leave the National Party in a minority.

**9.** Nelson Mandela had met with de Klerk. De Klerk respected Mandela and knew he needed Mandela's support to work out a solution to their country's problems.

## ■ TASK

The cards show some of the motives that people have suggested for de Klerk's extraordinary concessions in February 1990. Sort the cards into categories by listing:

**1.** Factors that were to do with the situation already existing.
**2.** Factors that were beyond de Klerk's control.
**3.** Factors that were to do with de Klerk's hopes for the future.

(Some factors may fit into more than one category.)

*123*

# The release of Nelson Mandela

Nelson Mandela was 72 years old in 1990. He had been in prison for 26 years. Mandela would not agree to be released until all his fellow prisoners had been released. Nor was he willing to be released just to get the National Party off the hook. He insisted that the ANC and other parties should be unbanned and that he was not going to retire. Walter Sisulu and the others were released in October 1989. Mandela walked out of jail in February 1990. He immediately captured the initiative by an extraordinary speech (Source 3).

**SOURCE 4** Nelson and Winnie Mandela, on his release from prison, February 1990

**SOURCE 3** An extract from Mandela's speech on his release

66 *Friends, Comrades, fellow South Africans. I greet you in the name of peace, democracy and freedom for all! I stand before you, not as a prophet but as a humble servant of you, the people. Your tireless and heroic sacrifices have made it possible for me to be here today. I therefore place the remaining years of my life in your hands.*

*Today, the majority of South Africans, black and white, recognise that apartheid has no future. It has to be ended by our own decisive mass action.*

*Mr de Klerk has gone further than any National politician in taking real steps to normalise the situation. However, there are further demands which have to be met before negotiations on the basic demands of our people can begin. I reiterate our call for an end to the State of Emergency and the freeing of all political prisoners. Negotiations for the dismantling of apartheid will have to address the overwhelming demand of our people for a democratic, non-racial and unitary South Africa. There must be an end to the white monopoly of political power.*

*Our struggle has reached a decisive moment. We call on our people to seize this moment so that progress towards democracy is rapid and uninterrupted. We have waited too long for our freedom. Now is the time to intensify the struggle on all fronts.* 99

**SOURCE 5** Mandela, writing in 1990

66 *Whites are fellow South Africans and we want them to feel safe and to know that we appreciate the contribution they have made towards the development of this country.* 99

**SOURCE 6** Mandela's report in 1994 of a conversation with F.W. de Klerk

66 *I told de Klerk that the ANC had not struggled against apartheid for seventy-five years only to yield to a disguised form of it. If it was his true intention to preserve apartheid through the Trojan Horse of group rights then he did not truly believe in ending apartheid.* 99

Mandela had clearly not abandoned his principles during the long years in prison, nor his readiness to fight. But it was not a call for revenge. Some white South Africans were horrified to be talked to like this, and called for his death. But many were charmed, reassured, even overwhelmed, to discover that he was not bitter. He offered them a place in a new South Africa.

1. Look at Sources 3–6. What words would you use to describe Nelson Mandela as he came out of prison and resumed politically active life?
2. What kind of South Africa did he want?
3. What would white South Africans think of him and what he said?
4. What would black South Africans think of him and what he said?
5. He was delighted to be free, but what problems did he face in putting his ideas into effect?

Even before his release, Mandela knew he faced some immediate problems: what would the attitude of the ANC be to someone who had not been able to be active in the party for so long? ANC leaders wanted to know how prison had affected him. Mandela was careful not to claim any special position in the party. Oliver Tambo was, after all, still officially leader. After discussions in Lusaka the ANC agreed that Mandela should replace Tambo, who had been seriously ill, in August 1990.

S**OURCE 7** Mandela and Tambo meet in Stockholm in 1990 after 27 years apart

## ■ TASK

1. On a copy of the timeline, Source 8, which your teacher will give you, mark:
a) in **blue**, items to do with the dismantling of apartheid
b) in **red**, items to do with moves towards a democratic South Africa
c) in **green**, items to do with violence.
2. Can you see any pattern to the violence?
3. How do you think the background of violence and death would affect the talks?

Source 8 shows the hectic pace of events. Apartheid was being dismantled; talks were going ahead to create a completely different kind of democratic government; there was enormous and terrifying violence. In the next two enquiries we will look at the talks and the violence, in that order, but it is important to remember that one was the background to the other.

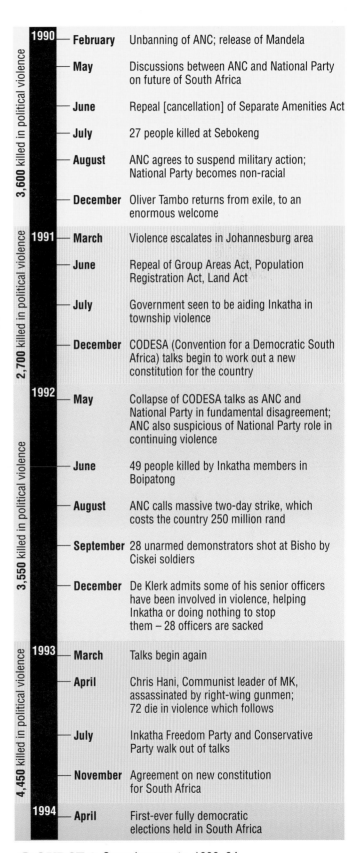

| | | |
|---|---|---|
| **1990** | **February** | Unbanning of ANC; release of Mandela |
| | **May** | Discussions between ANC and National Party on future of South Africa |
| | **June** | Repeal [cancellation] of Separate Amenities Act |
| | **July** | 27 people killed at Sebokeng |
| | **August** | ANC agrees to suspend military action; National Party becomes non-racial |
| | **December** | Oliver Tambo returns from exile, to an enormous welcome |
| **1991** | **March** | Violence escalates in Johannesburg area |
| | **June** | Repeal of Group Areas Act, Population Registration Act, Land Act |
| | **July** | Government seen to be aiding Inkatha in township violence |
| | **December** | CODESA (Convention for a Democratic South Africa) talks begin to work out a new constitution for the country |
| **1992** | **May** | Collapse of CODESA talks as ANC and National Party in fundamental disagreement; ANC also suspicious of National Party role in continuing violence |
| | **June** | 49 people killed by Inkatha members in Boipatong |
| | **August** | ANC calls massive two-day strike, which costs the country 250 million rand |
| | **September** | 28 unarmed demonstrators shot at Bisho by Ciskei soldiers |
| | **December** | De Klerk admits some of his senior officers have been involved in violence, helping Inkatha or doing nothing to stop them – 28 officers are sacked |
| **1993** | **March** | Talks begin again |
| | **April** | Chris Hani, Communist leader of MK, assassinated by right-wing gunmen; 72 die in violence which follows |
| | **July** | Inkatha Freedom Party and Conservative Party walk out of talks |
| | **November** | Agreement on new constitution for South Africa |
| **1994** | **April** | First-ever fully democratic elections held in South Africa |

*3,600 killed in political violence*
*2,700 killed in political violence*
*3,550 killed in political violence*
*4,450 killed in political violence*

S**OURCE 8** Some key events, 1990–94

# **W**hat problems were there in reaching agreement on democratic elections?

**F**.W. DE KLERK and Nelson Mandela had met and decided that they could trust one another. But could this personal respect lead to a new deal for all South Africans? Each faced problems of their own, as well as problems which emerged between them.

**S**OURCE 1 The first meeting of leading members of the National Party and the ANC, May 1990

### ■ TALKING POINTS

This next section is about the problems of reaching an agreement, but in fact the National Party and the ANC needed each other.

1. Why did the National Party need the ANC?
2. Why did the ANC need the National Party?

**S**OURCE 2 Nelson Mandela's view of de Klerk

*66 My first impression was that he was a man of integrity, a strong personality and, even more, a man who knows what he is doing and is determined to defend the new approach he is taking. We have developed enormous respect for each other and we talk very freely. 99*

## Problems between the ANC and the National Party

### ■ TASK

Three problems emerged in the negotiations. They are outlined in this box. As you go through them, imagine you are chairperson of the talks. What solution would you suggest for each of these problems?

### 1. Rival systems of election
Both the ANC and the National Party wanted to rule the new South Africa. For this reason the ANC insisted on 'simple' democracy – 'one person, one vote' – which would probably give them power. De Klerk tried to push for some system of power-sharing. He wanted minority parties, of which the National Party would probably be one, to have a share in power, to reassure whites that they would not be swamped.

### 2. Old enemies
■ The **National Party** had regarded the ANC as 'the enemy' for many years. Much of their

## Problems facing the National Party

1. De Klerk was trying to lead white South Africans away from over 40 years of apartheid and many more years of white supremacy. Could he take the majority of South African whites with him?
2. There was already opposition to change: the biggest group of white opponents de Klerk had to deal with was the Conservative Party, demanding a return to full apartheid.
3. Even more worrying were the various Nazi-style white racist groups, of which the most notorious was the Afrikaner Weerstandsbeweging (AWB), led by Eugene Terre'Blanche, who threatened to fight for a white South Africa.

However, de Klerk's position was greatly strengthened by a referendum (a vote) of the white electorate in March 1992. A massive 68 per cent vote in support of the direction he was taking took the wind out of the sails of most of his white opponents.

## Problems facing the ANC

1. The ANC had been banned since 1960. It had some secret membership inside South Africa and a small organisation based abroad. Yet it was trying to become the majority party in South Africa. It set out to recruit 2 million members by 1992, to build an organisation and meet the expectations of most black South Africans.
2. The ANC did not achieve its membership target. Young, angry blacks were not sure if the ANC was militant enough for them. Mandela was not sure he could control the militants. Many times his call for non-violence fell on deaf ears, especially when ANC members were being regularly attacked by Inkatha, the Zulu organisation, and the police.
3. Nelson Mandela's position was not made any easier by the actions of his wife, Winnie. Much younger than Nelson, Winnie Mandela had become a leader in her own right and a heroine to many young blacks. She spoke out against trusting de Klerk, in favour of violence. Several times Nelson supported her even when she was going against ANC policy. Then, in late 1990, she was charged with various serious offences, including killing the young activist Stompie Moeketsie. Nelson claimed it was all a plot to get at him through her. As the court heard more and more damning evidence against her, including misusing funds and having affairs while Mandela was in prison, he had to take notice. He announced their separation only eighteen months after leaving prison. It was a damaging episode.

propaganda had been directed towards showing that the ANC were Communists and terrorists. They particularly hated the Communists in the ANC leadership, such as Joe Slovo.

■ For the **ANC**, the National Party represented the men who, until recently, had ordered their imprisonment and the murder of their friends. It took great efforts on both sides to put the past behind them.

■ **The police and army.** Ever since 1948, the National Party had ensured that Afrikaners who shared their views filled senior positions in these forces. They were like the armed wing of the National Party and were not keen on

abandoning their prejudices. De Klerk quickly dismantled Botha's State Security Council and Joint Management Centres. Many police and army officers worried about their future.

### 5. Violence

All the time, the death toll mounted in township violence. Why wasn't de Klerk doing more to stop it, wondered the ANC leaders. What was he up to? Was he prolonging negotiations, hoping that the ANC would fall apart in conflicts between its moderate and militant members? Was he supporting Inkatha, the Zulu organisation led by Chief Buthelezi, as a rival to weaken the ANC?

## ■ TASK

Look at Sources 3–8. Which of the problems outlined on pages 126–27 do each of these sources link to?

**SOURCE 3** Van Tonder, of the Boerestaat Party, 1992

66 *As Israel is to the Jews, so the Transvaal, the Orange Free State and Natal are to the Afrikaner. They are our territory. We were the first to settle them. We trekked for them. We say, give it back.* 99

**SOURCE 4** AWB members at a pro-apartheid rally in September 1989, with a Nazi flag and their own swastika-like emblems

**SOURCE 5** A declaration by Eugene Terre'Blanche, leader of the AWB, in 1992

66 *No one dares take the land God gave us. We refuse to live under an ANC government. There will be war in South Africa. That day we will fight like our forefathers and we will fight until we win.* 99

**SOURCE 6** A comment by Walter Sisulu, of the ANC

66 *It is not easy for us to sit and negotiate. Many of the youngsters are not really interested in negotiations. They are very angry about the suffering they have gone through under apartheid.* 99

**SOURCE 7** A victim of violence in Natal describes what happened

66 *When I looked back I saw my son being struck with a huge knife. He was then thrown into the flames of our house which they had just torched. He was screaming but there was nothing I could do. To this day I can still hear the sizzling sound of the flames as they ate into my son's flesh.* 99

**SOURCE 8** Even at the opening meeting of the CODESA talks, in December 1991, the two leaders clashed. De Klerk attacked the ANC

66 *An organisation which remains committed to an armed struggle cannot be trusted completely when it also commits itself to peacefully negotiated solutions.* 99

Nelson Mandela lashed back

66 *I am gravely concerned about the behaviour of Mr de Klerk today. He has launched an attack on the ANC and in doing so he has been less than friendly. Even the head of an illegitimate, discredited minority regime as he, has certain moral standards to uphold. If a man can come to a conference and play this type of politics ... very few people would like to deal with such a man. We must make allowances for the fact that he is a product of apartheid.* 99

# Why was there so much violence in this period?

TRICKY AS THE negotiations were, they were conducted against a backdrop of terrible violence. People who were involved in politics were killed, but so were innocent people, including children. They were shot, burnt, chopped down with big knives called *pangas*, mutilated, disembowelled and disfigured. Killers regularly attacked people on commuter trains: 350 people were killed on trains between 1990 and 1993. Among the more notorious incidents of violence were:

■ Boipatong, June 1992. Inkatha members from migrant workers' compounds attacked residents of Boipatong black township, killing 49 people.
■ Bisho, September 1992. Unarmed ANC supporters marched in protest against Brigadier Gqozo, ruler of Ciskei homeland. He ordered his troops to open fire, killing 28 and wounding over 200 people.

SOURCE 1 Mandela, de Klerk, and Buthelezi meet in September 1991 to renounce violence. Despite their smiles, and although each leader promised to try to stop violence, little change actually took place

■ **TASK**

As you read through this enquiry, look for evidence of these four possible causes of the violence:

1. the effects of apartheid
2. the actions of Zulu leader Chief Buthelezi
3. the actions of the police and army – perhaps with National Party support
4. the actions of the ANC.

## Possible reasons for the violence

1. Was the violence simply the effect of apartheid? Certainly apartheid had taken a long and terrible toll on people's lives. Black people still lived in dire poverty near to white wealth. They were pushed around and humiliated by police. After a third-rate, under-funded education most young blacks had no hope for the future. Hopelessness breeds violence.
2. Was the Zulu organisation, Inkatha, and its leader, Buthelezi, to blame (see page 132)? In many areas organised violence took place between members of Inkatha and its rivals.
3. Were the police deliberately stirring up trouble, to try to destroy the peace process? As the violence began to spread and increase, victims reported that Inkatha members carried out their attacks while police looked on, did nothing, or even helped the attackers by providing transport. Were the police unbiased? On some occasions victims reported gangs of fighting men who were neither ANC comrades, nor Inkatha members, carrying out attacks on people and houses. They used unmarked vehicles and wore no uniform but their victims were always ANC supporters. Were the police actually taking part in the violence, as a 'Third Force'? And if so, who was giving them their orders? Did de Klerk know?

   Mandela and the ANC argued that de Klerk was still head of the government and should have done more to stop the violence. Some were suspicious of de Klerk's motives. If the government could split the blacks between the ANC and Inkatha, then the National Party might not be defeated. This was the main reason for the ANC walkout from the CODESA talks in May 1992. De Klerk always denied that his police were biased and protested that there was no 'Third Force'. However, even at the height of the violence, he continued to allow Zulus to carry 'cultural weapons' – shields, spears and sticks – even though this was highly provocative. Furthermore, some policemen gave disturbing evidence in court and to the media as Sources 6 and 7 on page 131 show.
4. Did the ANC use violence? For a long time Mandela denied this, but some of his colleagues did not have his scruples about violence.

*129*

S OURCE 2  Armed Zulu Inkatha supporters from migrant worker hostels in Katlehong township, 1991

S OURCE 3  An ANC comrade armed with a *panga*

**SOURCE 4** A statement in which Buthelezi appears to support violence, 1988

❝ *Inkatha believes it has a right to defend itself. We will not be intimidated out of existence. I am a black leader in the midst of violence. I am a leader of an angry people.* ❞

**SOURCE 5** Harry Gwala, ANC leader in Natal, speaking in 1992

❝ *Make no mistake, we kill Inkatha warlords. Why be apologetic about it, when they come to attack us, we offer them no Bibles. We believe in a just war. The difference between us and Inkatha is that we do not kill women and children. We hit hard on those who target us.* ❞

**SOURCE 6** A Sergeant Gibson told a BBC TV programme in 1991

❝ *Over the years we have been drilled with 'The ANC are terrorists' and this and this and this ... and now all of a sudden we've got to accept them as colleagues, which I find it hard to accept. I mean, I won't accept that.* ❞

**SOURCE 7** A white major in BOSS, Nico Basson, describes government involvement in violence

❝ *The government decided that black-on-black violence should be one of the strategies and a confrontation between Zulus and Xhosas should be encouraged because the two ethnic groups were the largest in the country. The army recruited people, especially youths, from outside South Africa, mainly rebel soldiers – trained them and sent them to protect compounds and start violence. They are trained to destabilise communities. The strategy is aimed at weakening the ANC and promoting Inkatha in its place.* ❞

**SOURCE 8** A comment made by Nelson Mandela in April 1993 on the ANC's role in the violence

❝ *There are members of the ANC who are killing our people. We must face the truth. It is true that the government is involved in the violence. It is members of the army, members of the police force, members of the intelligence service who are also behind this violence, because they want to cripple and weaken the ANC. But I am not going to criticise only the government and Inkatha. People who participate in this violence, for whatever reason – kill innocent people because others have killed innocent people – are not serving the cause of freedom.* ❞

1. What similarities and differences can you see in Sources 2 and 3?
2. What similarities and differences can you see in Sources 4 and 5?
3. Read Sources 6 and 7. Why would police and army officers try to sabotage the peace talks? What did they fear?
4. How reliable do you think Sources 6 and 7 are for finding out the truth about the 'Third Force'?
5. De Klerk set up an investigation, under Judge Goldstone, to look into accusations of a 'Third Force' with government support. Goldstone found that the police, army and even some ministers were involved in giving support to Inkatha. Foreign Minister Pik Botha and Justice Minister Adriaan Vlok admitted giving 250,000 rand to Buthelezi. Goldstone also found evidence that some army officers had encouraged violent attacks in order to sabotage the peace talks. A shocked de Klerk sacked 23 senior police and army officers in December 1992. How does this information affect your view of the reliability of Sources 6 and 7?
6. Read Source 8. Who does Nelson Mandela blame for the violence, in this source?
7. Which of the four reasons for the violence, given on page 129 does **each** of Sources 2–8 provide evidence to support?

## ■ ACTIVITY

### Judgement on Buthelezi

'Leader of his people' or 'Power-mad trouble-maker': which of these descriptions best fitted Mangosuthu Buthelezi during these years? Think about these two judgements as you work through the information and sources on the next two pages.

Mangosuthu Buthelezi (nicknamed 'Gatsha') was born in 1928 and was a member of the Youth League of the ANC from 1948–50. However, he left the ANC in order to get the white government's agreement to his becoming a chief. This took place in 1953. When the Bantustan policy got under way, Buthelezi was quite happy to be appointed as Chief Minister of the Zulu homeland of KwaZulu, with a salary of 11,400 rand a year (the average annual wage in KwaZulu was about 1500 rand a year).

To strengthen his position he revived Inkatha, a movement for Zulus founded in 1922. He claimed a million members, but there were no records of membership and no elections; Buthelezi liked to regard all Zulus as Inkatha members, automatically. As Zulus are the biggest single group of black South Africans, about 39 per cent of all blacks, this gave him great power. However, not all Zulus were Inkatha members: many were ANC supporters, including one of the other Zulu chiefs.

During the 1970s and 1980s, when the ANC was banned and black protest was weak, he was the most important black person in South Africa. He used different parts of his past to build up his position at different times – or even at the same time.

There were many blacks who hated him for his willingness to work with – and gain from – apartheid. He was stoned and jeered at by PAC supporters at the funeral of Robert Sobukwe in 1978, and Buthelezi never forgot it.

The unbanning of the ANC in 1990, and the approach of a new, democratic South Africa, spelt the end of his power. The ANC was committed to ending the homelands policy. If one's racial group counted for nothing in the proposed multi-racial South Africa, Buthelezi was not going to be as powerful as he had been. It soon became obvious that armed groups of Inkatha supporters were involved in violent attacks on other black people. This was happening in Natal, where many people were Zulu; it was also happening in Johannesburg, where Zulu migrant workers lived together in single-sex compounds.

> **SOURCE 9** In 1985 the South African newspaper *The Financial Mail* (a paper for business people) named Buthelezi 'Man of the Year'
>
> 66 *Who can deliver South Africa to a new era of conciliation and relative harmony? One name comes easily to mind: Chief Mangosuthu Buthelezi – a man of compromise . . . he is against violence . . . against sanctions . . . against consumer boycotts . . . a supporter of free market capitalism.* 99

He won support from traditional Zulus because of his ancestry.

He claimed to support non-violent protest after the ANC had abandoned it in 1960.

He claimed black support by referring to his ANC past and 'the struggle' against apartheid.

He liked the support he got from apartheid leaders as a strong black leader who was willing to work with them.

**SOURCE 10** Chief Buthelezi in 'traditional' Zulu costume

**SOURCE 11** The views of Buthelezi on the 1986 school boycotts

❝ *There is no black person who can condone the inadequacies which black children suffer from as far as the South African education system is concerned. When Coloured children, followed by Indian children, launched the boycott, I perfectly understood. When black children did so later, I sympathised. But when school boycotts were being used by exiles and their supporters in South Africa to get at me, I was opposed.* ❞

**SOURCE 12** Rich Mkhondo, a black reporter in South Africa, describes conditions in the migrant workers' hostels in 1991

❝ *Hostel inmates were forced to live in squalid conditions without day-to-day contact with normal family life. They were caged in dreadful, maze-like single-storey complexes for eleven months a year, going back to the homelands to renew their contracts each December.*

*Their bungalows were filthy and cold and greeted everyone with an unbearable stench. Heaps of rubbish littered the floors. There was no heating system in the cold winters. Rows of concrete bunks served as beds, with personal belongings tucked under them or hung on the walls. As many as sixteen men shared one big bungalow. Some hostels had no hot water, some had no water at all. No attempt was made by the authorities to improve conditions.* ❞

8. Use Sources 9–12 to describe how Buthelezi had become so famous and successful
9. Which sources show him making the most of his Zulu history?
10. How does Source 11 show his two-sidedness?
11. Why was Buthelezi so popular with white South Africans in the 1980s?
12. Why did so many black people hate him?
13. Why did the changes which began in 1990 present a threat to him?
14. Who was to blame for the conditions described in Source 12?
15. How did these conditions affect the situation in the townships?

■ **TASK**

**What were the reasons for violence?**

1. On your own copy of the table below, record whether you agree or disagree with the statements given, and the evidence that you have used to come to this decision.

| Statement | Agree/disagree | Evidence |
|---|---|---|
| Black people wanted revenge for the oppression of apartheid. | | |
| Young blacks were bitter about their lack of opportunities. | | |
| Young blacks were angry at the slow pace of change. | | |
| Conditions in miners' hostels were so bad that they were driven to violence. | | |
| Buthelezi encouraged his Inkatha supporters to attack ANC members as he feared the growing strength of the ANC. | | |
| Blacks attacked other blacks who had worked with the apartheid system. | | |
| Police acted as a 'Third Force' helping Inkatha members attack ANC members. | | |
| National Party leaders encouraged Inkatha in order to weaken the position of the ANC. | | |
| De Klerk did not give support to the 'Third Force'. | | |
| The ANC used violence to protect its own supporters. | | |
| The ANC used violence against its rivals | | |

2. Do you think any of the four reasons presented in this enquiry as possible causes of the violence were wrong or unimportant?
3. Which of the four do you think was most important?
4. How do you think two or more of the four causes were linked?

*133*

# Democracy at last

SOURCE 1 Joe Slovo (left) and Chris Hani

SOURCE 2 South Africans queuing to vote in the elections of April 1994

VIOLENCE AND DISAGREEMENT continued after the talks began again in March 1993. In April, Chris Hani, the popular black Communist leader of MK, was assassinated by white right-wing fanatics. In July a group of right-wingers, including Inkatha and the Conservative Party, walked out of the talks.

The National Party still wanted some protection for themselves and their followers if simple 'one person, one vote' democracy was introduced. It was a suggestion of Joe Slovo, once the man white South Africans hated most, that provided the solution:

- guarantee the jobs of all civil servants, police and army who had served the apartheid government
- have a power-sharing system for five years. Any party with over 20 per cent of the votes would have the right to appoint a Deputy President; any party with over 5 per cent of the vote would have the right to appoint a member of the government.

On this basis the country prepared for an election in April 1994. Buthelezi refused to take part until the last minute, but then agreed that Inkatha would stand. So, eventually, did the white Conservatives.

The ruler of the homeland called Bophuthatswana, seeing his power coming to an end, tried to prevent his people from taking part. His government employees went on strike and AWB members went to support him. They arrived in 'Bop' and began shooting at any black person they saw. This led the Bop army to mutiny against their ruler and the AWB gunmen were shot down.

It seemed a grave warning of white violence to come, but the election passed off peacefully. Twenty million people waited patiently to vote, most of them for the first time in their lives. The result was victory for the ANC, with 62.5 per cent of the vote. Nelson Mandela became President. But, with 20.5 per cent, the National Party gained the right to appoint de Klerk as a Deputy President. Inkatha, which got 10.5 per cent, gained the right for Buthelezi to become a minister in Mandela's government.

SOURCE 3 De Klerk offers Mandela his congratulations

*** He has walked a long road and now stands on the top of the hill. The journey is never complete and, as he contemplates the next hill, I hold out my hand to him in friendship and co-operation. ***

SOURCE 4 An extract from Mandela's speech at his inauguration as President

*** Out of the experience of an extraordinary human disaster which was allowed to go on far too long, must be born a society of which all humanity will be proud. We pledge ourselves to liberate all our people from the continuing bondage of poverty, deprivation, suffering, gender and other discrimination. Never, never and never again shall it be that this beautiful land will again experience the oppression of one by another. The sun will never set on so glorious a human achievement. Let freedom reign. God bless Africa. ***

**1.** Nelson Mandela called the result 'a small miracle'. What do you think he meant?

**S**OURCE 5 President Mandela, celebrating with his Deputy Presidents: on the left, F. W. de Klerk (National Party), and on the right, Thabo Mbeki (ANC), May 1994

## ■ ACTIVITY

So bloody war was avoided and a democratic solution reached. Who do you think deserves the credit for this? Obviously lots of people. Here are some of them:

Nelson Mandela

F.W. de Klerk

Joe Slovo

Anyone else?

Chief Buthelezi

National Party negotiators

ANC negotiators

White voters

Black South Africans

All South Africans

Choose the three people (or groups) you would nominate for your own 'Peace Prize'. Write a sentence on each explaining your choice.

# Has South Africa beaten the legacy of apartheid?

THE 1994 ELECTIONS seemed a dream ending to a terrible situation: millions of South Africans of all races queued patiently to vote; the result was not only that the revered Nelson Mandela became President, but also that whites and blacks who were not supporters of the ANC shared power. But history isn't a movie that ends and you all leave the cinema and get on with real life. History *is* real life, and it goes on. What happened after the 1994 election?

## The Truth and Reconciliation Commission

As we have seen in this book, South Africa was a deeply divided society. These divisions went back far beyond the beginning of apartheid in 1948. Black people had been killed by white settlers and had their land taken away from them; whites had fought and killed each other in the South African War. Then in the last years of apartheid violence had reached new heights. Could all this just be forgotten?

Archbishop Desmond Tutu (see Source 1) thought not. He argued that people needed to face what he called 'the beast of the past' (Source 2). The new government set up the Truth and Reconciliation Commission (TRC), chaired by Archbishop Tutu.

**SOURCE 1** Archbishop Desmond Tutu with the report of the Truth and Reconciliation Commission, October 1998

There were two sides to their task:

- to listen to the stories of people, black or white, who had been injured, or lost relatives, in the violence between 1960 and 1994. Government control of press and TV in the last years of apartheid meant that the truth about the violence was not reported accurately. The Commission travelled all over the country to allow people to describe openly what had happened. By listening to them in public, the Commission gave them a voice, valued their suffering and perhaps helped them to move their lives on. Sources 3 and 4 are just two of the thousands of stories they heard
- to offer amnesty (pardon) to those who had committed violent acts, if they came forward and told the truth. In many cases, torturers faced their victims, killers faced the close relatives of the person they had killed, and asked for forgiveness. Sometimes they received it.

## SOURCE 2 Archbishop Tutu explains the purpose of the TRC

*" Having looked the beast of the past in the eye, having asked and received forgiveness and having made amends, let us shut the door on the past – not in order to forget it, but in order not to allow it to imprison us. Let us move into the glorious future of a new kind of society where people count, not because of biological irrelevancies . . . but because they are persons of infinite worth created in the image of God. "*

1. Why does Tutu call the past 'a beast'?
2. Why might it be important to let those who have suffered speak?

## ■ TALKING POINTS

1. If someone had killed a close relative of yours, would you want to meet them? What would you feel? What would you say?
2. Is it right to offer amnesty to killers who confess to their crime?

## SOURCE 3 An extract from the South African Press Association report on the TRC, 29 April 1996

*" CHURCH STREET BOMB SURVIVOR WANTS JUSTICE*
*James Simpson was injured by a car-bomb on 20 May 1983, in Church St, Pretoria, probably planted by the ANC, which killed nineteen people. Simpson told the Truth and Reconciliation Commission that he had been working in his office when the bomb went off. Shards of window glass had sprayed across the room, cutting his face and leaving splinters in his eyes. 'When I got to the street I saw cars burning and injured people lying around. My sympathies are with the injured who have never fully recovered.'*

*In order to forgive the bombers, Simpson said, he needed to know who they were. The two men who planted the bomb were killed in the explosion. Asked by Commission chairman Archbishop Tutu what he wanted for the people who ordered the bombing, Simpson said 'Simply that they would admit they gave the orders'. "*

## SOURCE 4 From the South African Press Association report on the TRC, 30 April 1996

*" POLICE KILLED MY HUSBAND, WIDOW TELLS TRUTH COMMISSION*
*The widow of Suluman Saloojee, who died in police custody in 1964, said his death had left her with a lingering hatred for some whites. 'If I see a white policeman I hate him, I am sorry to say,' Rokoya Saloojee told the Truth and Reconciliation Commission on the second day of its hearings in Johannesburg.*

*Suluman Saloojee, a 32-year-old solicitor's clerk, was active in the Transvaal Indian Congress and the ANC. He was detained by police on 6 July 1964 and on 9 September allegedly fell to his death from the seventh floor of police headquarters. The inquest into Saloojee's death lasted just five minutes, Rokoya said. The magistrates had not allowed her to ask questions and said 'That is all' when she asked why her husband's clothes were full of blood. "*

3. From your reading of this book, what events would you want the TRC to hear about?
4. What do you think the witnesses in Sources 3 and 4 gained from talking to the TRC?
5. What did other South Africans gain from hearing or reading about them?
6. Do you think Tutu's aims for the TRC, in Source 2, will be met?

## What happened to the government?

Apartheid left South Africa with enormous problems. There were huge inequalities in wealth, leading to problems in housing, education and health. One of the legacies of the violence was a tremendously high crime rate. Black South Africans pinned high hopes on Nelson Mandela to deal with these inequalities and improve their situation. For many, he seemed to move too slowly. On the other hand, Mandela and the ANC moved too fast for many whites. Former National Party President de Klerk, who became a Deputy President after the 1994 elections, resigned from the government in 1996.

# ■ ACTIVITY

How will we judge the new South Africa? When you read this, the story of South Africa will have moved on from when I stopped writing in 1999. At the moment it seems to me that the important issues are:

■ is the government dealing with the inequalities in housing, education and health that apartheid produced?
■ are there still high levels of violent crime?
■ is South Africa still a multiracial democracy?

This is my verdict on Nelson Mandela's 1994–99 government for some of these issues.

### Education

There are still huge inequalities in the education available to black and white children; a few black children have been admitted to white schools; there has been lots of talk – little action; no money has been available for education – so there is a gross shortage of textbooks. Verdict: 3 out of 10.

### Democracy

Free, peaceful and democratic elections were held again in 1999. The results are shown in Source 5. As you can see, the ANC won overwhelmingly. In fact they only just fell short of achieving 66.67 per cent of the vote, or two-thirds, which would have allowed them to change the constitution of South Africa, if they had wanted to. Their opponents were divided, with the National Party, in power from 1948 to 1994 (and now called the New National Party) winning only a handful of seats. Nelson Mandela retired and the new President, Thabo Mbeki (see Source 5 on page 135), promised 'to build a South Africa which truly belongs to all who live in it'. My only doubt is that there is no real opposition to the ANC. Verdict: 9 out of 10.

### What is your verdict now?

How well do you think the South African government is dealing with these issues now? What mark out of ten would **you** give them? Are there new problems that they need to tackle now?

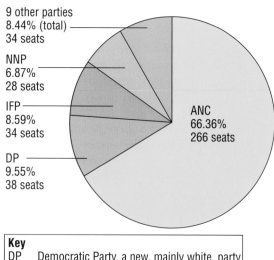

**Key**
DP    Democratic Party, a new, mainly white, party
IFP   Inkatha Freedom Party, led by Buthelezi
NNP  New National Party

S OURCE 5  Election results, 1999

# ■ TASK

### What have you learned from this book?

I hope you have learned a lot from this book, but here are some thoughts about things you have learned which could apply to other situations apart from South Africa. In each case, think about an example from this book, then try to think of another example from other historical topics you have studied.

■ People use events from past history to help explain the present: sometimes they choose good examples, but sometimes they find stories which seem to support bad action.
■ People are capable of treating each other in horrible ways.
■ In the twentieth century, problems in one country involved the rest of the world. We are all part of one world and cannot ignore each other.
■ Having the right to vote is very important.
■ People will resist being humiliated and downtrodden and there are different ways of doing this. In this resistance, individuals can make a difference.
■ People are capable of reconciliation, of forgiving and talking their way out of their problems.
■ Learning about the past helps you to understand the present.

# Glossary

**AFRICAN NATIONAL CONGRESS (ANC)** a protest organisation formed in 1912 to unite all blacks in protest against white rule; it was known as the South African Native National Congress (SANNC) until 1923. Initially its members were all black Africans but white people were able to join later

**AFRICANIST** someone who believes that black African people should feel pride in themselves and their history, and try to overcome white rule without help from any other racial group

**APARTHEID** means 'separateness'. It was a system of government set up in 1948, in which people were treated differently according to the colour of their skin

**ASYLUM** a place of safety, where someone can be protected

**BANNING ORDERS** orders issued by the police, which aimed to prevent opponents of apartheid from meeting other people who shared their views, or from broadcasting or publishing their views

**BANTU** the name for the black people who moved into southern Africa between AD300 and AD1000. Later it was used by supporters of apartheid to mean all black Africans; it is regarded as an insult by black people

**BANTUSTANS** the term used by the apartheid government for the ten black 'homelands' where all blacks were eventually supposed to live

**BLACK CONSCIOUSNESS** a movement that encouraged black people to take pride in themselves and their history, and not to feel inferior to whites (*see also* Africanist)

**BOER** an Afrikaans word meaning 'farmer'; it is often used to describe all Dutch settlers and their descendants in South Africa

**BROEDERBOND** a secret organisation for Afrikaners, set up in 1918; its aim was to help Afrikaners and oppose British, or English-speaking, rule

**BUREAU OF STATE SECURITY (BOSS)** the South African secret police

**CAPITALISM** an economic system in which private companies and individuals create wealth

**CODESA** Convention for a Democratic South Africa, negotiations which began in 1991 to decide what form of elections and government South Africa should have in future

**COLONY** land outside a country's borders but which is owned by it. Colonies were usually less developed countries seized or conquered by more developed ones for military, economic or other reasons

**COLOUREDS** the name used in South Africa for people with parents or ancestors from different races, for example, a white father and a black mother

**COMMONWEALTH** an international organisation made up of Britain and many of the countries that were once part of the British Empire

**COMMUNISM** a system in which the state owns all economic activity, the benefits of which are shared out equally to create a classless society

**CONCENTRATION CAMP** a prison camp where lots of people were collected together, often under very harsh conditions

**CONSTITUTION** the rules which govern how a country should be run: for example, how governments should be elected; the legal rights people have as citizens, etc.

**DECOLONISATION** a process in which the government of a colony is handed back to the people whose ancestors have always lived there, instead of being governed by more recent settlers

*DIFAQANE* 'forced migration': a word used in some African languages to describe the disruption of traditional society in southern Africa in the early 1800s (*see also MFECANE*)

**ECONOMIC DEPRESSION** a time when trade and investment in businesses is declining, resulting in high unemployment

**ETHNIC GROUP** a group of people who share the same race, language and traditions

**EXILE** being forced to leave one's home or country

**GREAT TREK** the journey which some Boers set out on in 1836, leaving the Cape to settle lands in the interior of southern Africa

**GUERRILLAS** fighters who carry out undercover attacks, against government targets for example

**INDUSTRIAL REVOLUTION** the process in which first Britain, in the late eighteenth and early nineteenth centuries, and then other countries began to develop large-scale industries such as manufacturing, leading to the growth of towns and massive social change

**INFLUX CONTROL** the apartheid policy of restricting the numbers of black people allowed to live and work in cities

**INKATHA** a political organisation for Zulus, led by Chief Buthelezi

**JOINT MANAGEMENT CENTRES** Local organisations run by a police chief or senior army officer, to control the population

**KHOI** herders who were living in southern Africa at least 3,000 years ago

**MANDATE** a territory under the protection of the League of Nations, an international organisation that existed in the 1920s and 1930s; mandates were handed over to various member countries, which governed them on behalf of the League (and later the United Nations)

*MFECANE* 'crushing'; a word used in some African languages to describe the disruption of traditional society in southern Africa in the early 1800s (*see also DIFAQANE*)

**MIGRANT LABOUR SYSTEM** a system in which labourers were encouraged to leave their farms to work for several months at a time in the mines and other industries; wages were low but they were given food and lodgings

**MK** the abbreviation for Umkhonto we Sizwe ('Spear of the Nation'), the military wing of the African National Congress

**PAN AFRICAN CONGRESS (PAC)** a black nationalist organisation formed by Robert Sobukwe in 1959

**PASS SYSTEM** a system first introduced by Dutch settlers to control the movement of black workers, and extended under apartheid; black people had to carry a pass giving personal details and information about their employer

**PETTY APARTHEID** laws governing separation of the races in lots of minor ways, especially those laws brought in under the Separate Amenities Act of 1953, which prevented blacks and whites from using the same public transport, parks, shops, beaches, etc.

**Poqo** 'We alone', the military wing of the Pan African Congress

**Prospectors** people who search for deposits of gold or other valuable minerals

**Rand** the South African currency

**Repealed** officially withdrawn

**Republic** a form of government in which the supreme authority (the president) is elected by the people (instead of inheriting his or her position, as a king or queen does)

**Reservations** areas of land where blacks were allowed to own or rent property

**San** hunter-gatherers who were living in southern Africa at least 3,000 years ago; they were hunted to extinction in South Africa by whites

**Sanctions** punishments or rules designed to make people behave in a different way

**Segregation** separation into different groups; in South Africa people were segregated according to their racial group

**Socialism** a system in which most economic activity (factories, farms, banks, transport) is owned and run by the government for the benefit of everyone. Also, more simply, a belief that wealth should be divided equally between everyone

**South African Defence Force (SADF)** the South African army

**State Security Council** a group of army generals and police chiefs, set up in 1982 by P.W. Botha to advise him on policy

**Subsistence** producing food mainly for your own consumption, not to sell to others

**Suffrage** the right to vote

**Truth and Reconciliation Commission** a committee led by Archbishop Desmond Tutu, set up after the 1994 elections in South Africa so that the truth about the crimes committed during the apartheid years could be told

**Umkhonto we Sizwe** 'Spear of the Nation', the military wing of the ANC, usually abbreviated to MK

**United Democratic Front (UDF)** a group of over 500 smaller organisations, set up in 1985 to co-ordinate resistance to Prime Minister Botha's constitutional reforms

**United Nations** an international organisation set up in 1945 that works to promote peace and justice around the world

**Xhosa** an ethnic group of black Africans from the south-eastern area of South Africa

**Zulu** the largest ethnic group of black Africans, from eastern South Africa

## The Schools History Project

Set up in 1972 to bring new life to history for students aged 13–16, the Schools History Project continues to play an innovatory role in secondary history education. From the start, SHP aimed to show how good history has an important contribution to make to the education of a young person. It does this by creating courses and materials which both respect the importance of up-to-date, well-researched history and provide enjoyable learning experiences for students.

Since 1978 the Project has been based at Trinity and All Saints University College Leeds. It continues to support, inspire and challenge teachers through the annual conference, regional courses and website: http://www.schoolshistoryproject.org.uk. The Project is also closely involved with government bodies and awarding bodies in the planning of courses for Key Stage 3, GCSE and A level.

### Series consultant
Terry Fiehn

Note: the wording and sentence structure of some written sources have been adapted and simplified to make them accessible to all students, while faithfully preserving the sense of the original.

# Index